UNDAUNTED

LIVING FIERCELY INTO CLIMATE MELTDOWN IN
AN AUTHORITARIAN WORLD

CAROLYN BAKER

APOCRYPHILE
PRESS

Apocryphile Press
PO Box 255
Hannacroix, NY 12087
www.apocryphilepress.com

Copyright © 2022 by Carolyn Baker

Printed in the United States of America
ISBN 978-1-955821-91-9 | paper
ISBN 978-1-955821-92-6 | ePub

No part of this book may be reproduced, stored in a retrieval system, or transmitted in any form or by any means—electronic, mechanical, photocopy, recording, or otherwise—without written permission of the author and publisher, except for brief quotations in printed reviews.

Please join our mailing list at www.apocryphilepress.com/free. We'll keep you up-to-date on all our new releases, and we'll also send you a FREE BOOK. Visit us today!

ALSO BY THE AUTHOR

- The Journey of Forgiveness
- Coming Out of Fundamentalist Christianity
- Sacred Demise
- Navigating the Coming Chaos
- Collapsing Consciously
- Collapsing Consciously eBook Meditations
- Love in the Age of Ecological Apocalypse
- Return to Joy (with Andrew Harvey)
- Dark Gold: The Human Shadow and the Global Crisis
- Savage Grace (with Andrew Harvey)
- Journey to the Promised Land: How a Homeless Stranger Took Me Home
- Saving Animals from Ourselves (with Andrew Harvey)
- Radical Regeneration (with Andrew Harvey)
- Confronting Christofascism: Healing the Evangelical Wound

If we fall in love with creation deeper and deeper,
we will respond to its endangerment with passion.

Hildegard of Bingen
12th Century Mystic

CONTENTS

FOREWORD

Jack D. Forbes, professor emeritus and former chair of Native American Studies at the University of California Davis, in his book, *Columbus and Other Cannibals*, wrote thirty years ago about what he called the wétiko (cannibal) disease, something he also referred to as the "sickness of exploitation."

As a Native American, Forbes was intimately acquainted with living in the wake of and within continuing forms of genocide, erasure, and oppression from the U.S. government and its societal programming.

Cannibalism, as Forbes defined it, "is the consuming of another's life for one's own private purpose or profit."

"Imperialism and exploitation are forms of cannibalism and, in fact, are precisely those forms of cannibalism which are most diabolical or evil," he wrote. "Few, if any, societies on the face of the Earth have ever been as avaricious, cruel, violent, and aggressive as have certain European populations."

Native Americans experienced wétiko in brutal fashion not long after "first contact" with Europeans.

A few years ago, I had a long conversation with a friend

who is a Chiricahua Apache elder. He prefers to remain anonymous nowadays, so I won't include his name here, but he told me:

"The white man slaughtered, during one short period alone, 50 million buffalo, because thousands of us relied on them, and in less than a generation, they annihilated them. And they take pride in this, and take pictures of the dead buffalo, like it takes a real man to shoot an animal with a high-powered rifle from far away."

To emphasize what he was saying, he went on to say that when Native Americans talk about "great" people, they usually speak of medicine people or people who engage in acts of self-less generosity, "but all of the 'greats' that the whites ever write about were great at destruction and subjugating people." Insert name of U.S. military general or corporation or political leader here.

Ella Cara Deloria (1889–1971) was born on the Yankton Reservation in South Dakota and grew up in a prominent family on the Standing Rock reservation. She studied at Columbia University with Franz Boas and became an ethnologist, authoring numerous books.

In one of them, *Waterlily*, posthumously published in 1988, she wrote of an old tradition in pre-contact Native American culture called "fellowhood, a solemn friendship pact that must endure forever."

How she described this is worth quoting at length, as it is the concept I wish to use as a contrast to our present-tense converging crises generated by hundreds of years of wétiko society.

"Fellows were men of comparable standing and ability who were drawn together by like tastes and by a mutual respect and admiration for each other's character and personal charm. 'The best I have is for my fellow' was their code from the time they pledged eternal loyalty. In line with that, one's best horse automatically went to the other whenever they met after a prolonged separation. When possible, they went on the warpath together in order to protect each other. In every phase of life they must act without thought of self, in defense of and to the advantage of the other. One must give one's life to save the other. Fellowhood was a compelling association whose obligations were a pleasure.

"Two men who became fellows, *kola*, immediately thereby placed themselves in the limelight, fully cognizant that others watched them, as if saying, 'Well, so they think themselves worthy of so high a calling, do they? We shall see how they will measure up!' For men of doubtful stature who became *kola* without counting the cost soon petered out and became the butt of many jokes and the derision of men. It was no wonder that instances of fellowhood were not common, since much thought was needed before taking the step.

"The demands on fellows were somewhat greater even than those on natural brothers, loyal and devoted as brothers were supposed to be. And automatically, like brothers, each fellow was son to the other's parents and father to his children. All other relatives were likewise shared. Each was brother-in-law to the other's wife, but with this difference: whereas an informality, marked by joking and taking one another in an offhand manner, was ordinarily permitted between brother- and sister-in-law, men in fellowhood must respect and venerate the other's wife like a sister[1]"

Could the disparity between wétiko culture and authentic Indigenous culture possibly be any greater?

Ella Cara's nephew, Vine Deloria Jr. (1933-2005), was a Native American scholar, attorney, and author of more than two dozen books, including *Custer Died for Your Sins*; *God is Red*; *Power and Place*; *Red Earth, White Lies*; and *Spirit and Reason*.

In his book, *We Talk, You Listen: New Tribes, New Turf*, he prophetically, wrote this:

> Eventually the land upon which people live determines how they will live. Before the coming of the white man the land was untouched [in the way it is today]. It provided for everyone and people dared not disturb it since it was the property of all. There was no need for industry or tedious work, since the land provided.

This is not to say the land was left alone. People had a close, intimate relationship to it, listening to its needs rather than imposing their own.

Waterlily relates how, in a time of need, a buffalo dreamer in a tribe would call on his brothers, the buffalo, who would then arrive to give of themselves in order to feed the people. As soon as enough kills were made to provide what was needed, the tribal leaders called a halt. "Stop! It is enough. Our friends have kept their vow; once again they have given themselves to save us; once again they have extended hospitality to us. Let us kill no more than we need. It is enough," Ella Cara wrote.

This form of responsible relationship carries forward into interrelationships with *all* animals, plants, and landscapes.

> Over a period of four hundred years the white man has completely changed the land. But the land has not given up its powers. Today society is almost completely industrialized and the land is almost completely settled. Yet the wealth of natural resources and technological innovations has created a type of society that does not require tedious work. However, everyone will be forced to live in small tribal groups because that will be the only way to survive.
>
> Thus, whether the land is developed or not, and

whether the people desire it or not, the land determines the forms by which societies are able to live on this continent. An undeveloped land created tribes and a fully developed land is creating tribes. In essence Indians have really won the battle for cultural survival. It remains only for years to go by and the rise of youth to continue, and everyone will be in the real mainstream of American life—the tribe.[2]

That book was published more than half a century ago, in 1970. Given what the Indigenous people of this continent have endured since first contact, it should not come as a surprise that Vine Deloria Jr.'s books presaged the converging crises that are besetting the entire planet today. Indeed, from his perspective, they were written in the aftermath of Native American cultures' externally induced catastrophe and now their ongoing survivance beneath the weight of colonization and wétiko culture.

While I was working on my book *The End of Ice*, I had the privilege of meeting Wesley Aiken, one of the town elders of Utqiagvik, the northernmost town in Alaska, situated right on the coast of the Arctic Ocean. He has since passed away, but Wesley was 92 years old when I met with him the summer of 2017. Having seen his way of life dramatically altered by colonization, wétiko, and runaway climate disruption, at the end of a lengthy conversation, he told me this:

Some people from the lower forty-eight and the rest of the world are worrying about us, but I don't know why, because we are not worried. We know this [runaway climate disruption] is happening. People before me were telling us this was going to happen. They knew. I don't know how they knew, but they knew. I listened to them. Then it started to happen.

And now, I just know it's happening, and I don't think it's going to stop.

Again, it should come as no surprise that when Aiken's elders, and their elders, saw the white colonists infected with wétiko, it was not difficult for them to predict where it would lead society—and the planet itself.

Undaunted: Living Fiercely into Climate Meltdown in an Authoritarian World is Carolyn Baker's generous gift to us all, during this time of converging crises. Coming from a former psychotherapist who has been keenly attuned to social and ecological breakdown across the planet for decades, this book is a basket of psychological, spiritual, and intellectual tools, offered during a time when we need them as much as food and water.

In the introduction she writes: "Specifically, this book is a call, an invitation, a heartfelt plea to commit to the inner work and external Earth and human stewardship that climate chaos and authoritarian encroachment on our humanity is demanding of us, and to do it fiercely."

It is time for all of us to listen, then act upon what Indigenous peoples across this continent have been saying and practicing as a way of life for millennia. Not because it is a practical means of survival in this era of the collapse of western so-called civilization, but because it is the right thing to do.

The book you are holding will aid you in getting started on this.

Dahr Jamail
March 2022
Port Townsend, Washington

INTRODUCTION

The word *undaunted* is easily misinterpreted to mean *invincible* or *implacable*; that is, *incapable of being extinguished or made extinct*. In reality, it simply means *not intimidated or discouraged by difficulty, danger, or disappointment*. More accurately, it means *indomitable, steadfast, undeterred, audacious, courageous, undismayed*, or *unfaltering*. To be undaunted does not mean that one will never be discouraged or feel like giving up. It does not even mean that one will survive.

To live undaunted in the face of climate catastrophe in a world that is also becoming increasingly autocratic is an arduous task, even on a very good day. What is more, to live *fiercely* in such a domain may even sound preposterous. However, fierceness does not mean being barbarous, rageful, or cruel. Rather, to live fiercely means *to live passionately, to demand excellence, and to live inclusively, honestly, and authentically*. Equally significant, it means to live *into*, not away from— or in spite of—what feels overwhelming. Living *into* means knowing what one's future and the future of the planet is likely to be, yet intentionally choosing to live passionately *into* a scenario that is unprecedented and terrifying for human beings.

I am not a climate scientist, but I have been studying climate research for more than fifteen years. Nevertheless, this book is not about climate science. We are inundated with gargantuan quantities of climate research, yet our planet appears to be in climate hospice because humanity has refused to undergo the treatment that climate research reveals might put its malady into remission. We may have endless *fantasies* about "fighting" or "reversing" or "mitigating" climate catastrophe, but the *fact* is that runaway, unprecedented global warming is so calamitous, that to avoid cataclysm, humanity would need to alter its living arrangements to an extent that humans are not willing to even consider.

Using the words "climate change" to describe the situation is becoming increasingly absurd. Therefore, I resist using the words "climate change" because the status of Earth's climate now defies the word "change." The tipping points we have passed on a trajectory toward extinction are nothing less than breathtaking—no pun intended.

So, this book will not be a regurgitation of climate science replete with charts, graphs, or tables depicting ice melt. There will be no discussion of methane burps or flooding landscapes even as our bodies and souls are regularly "flooded" with horror regarding the eco-extremes exploding on our planet. "Climate chaos" is the term I will be using throughout this book to describe our global climate predicament, for it can no longer be neatly mapped or predicted. One definition of *chaos* is *behavior so unpredictable as to appear random, owing to great sensitivity to small changes in conditions.* Climate chaos is now our day-to-day reality.

Specifically, this book is a call, an invitation, a heartfelt plea to commit to the inner work and external Earth and human stewardship that climate chaos and authoritarian encroachment on our humanity is demanding of us. And to do it fiercely! Nothing in these pages guarantees a positive outcome. Rather, my focus is on nature's invitation and our response, rather than on the end result of our efforts. The issue is not how it turns out, but how we turn up.

My friend and colleague, Michael Dowd, sometimes calls himself a "collapse chaplain." I fully embrace that label for myself. Since 2009, my work has focused on assisting humanity in facing our global predicament, which (I must once again remind us) is not a series of problems to be solved, but a set of circumstances to which we can only respond, because Earth's environment has passed so many tipping points that the "problems" are now unsolvable. As stated above, we may now be in a state of planetary hospice, but even if we are, this should not dissuade us from standing undaunted and living fiercely. You will understand why that is so if you read the following pages.

If all of this sounds like gloom and doom, well it is—except that that is not the whole story. Many people who understand climate science and our global predicament *are* living in a state of doom—either bitterly and angrily resigning themselves to human extinction or deeply immersing themselves in climate activism or techno-fixes which they believe will reverse what cannot be reversed.

Another group of people are living in a "post-doom" reality because they have accepted climate chaos and the ensuing collapse of systems that accompanies it. This book is a post-doom manual that painstakingly invites the reader to consider the *benefits* of accepting our planetary predicament—benefits one cannot experience unless one accepts it.

One of those benefits is living undaunted and fiercely even

while we are wide awake to our unwanted—but likely —future.

In a recent conversation with Michael Dowd, environmental activist and energy specialist Karen Perry outlined a number of benefits people can experience by accepting our predicament. Perry created her list after conducting many conversations with people deeply concerned with climate chaos and the collapse of systems. She invites all of us to compose our own lists as we cultivate acceptance.[1]

More than a decade ago, when I wrote my book *Navigating the Coming Chaos*, I was one of the first authors to talk about the emotional impacts of our predicament. In those days, if anyone had approached a psychotherapist about the issue of climate anxiety or climate grief, they may well have been pathologized as depressed, hysterical, or suicidal.

Yet now, even as I have been writing this book, a Sunday *New York Times* article, "Climate Change Enters the Therapy Room," reveals that, "Eco-anxiety, a concept introduced by young activists, has entered a mainstream vocabulary. And professional organizations are hurrying to catch up, exploring approaches to treating anxiety that is both existential and, many would argue, rational."[2]

In a recent interview with Michael Dowd, "Living Well Now," he states that "Confusion and collective insanity reign without a life-centered view of ecology, energy and history."[3] In the following pages, I offer a portion of that wisdom with emphasis on *how we can accept our wildly uncertain future by living fiercely into it.*

Each chapter of the book concludes with a series of "Fierce Practices"—simple but profound tools that readers can utilize to assist them as they perform the inner work that post-doom living demands. Many folks are willing to spend several hours a day gardening, canning, learning off-the-grid living skills, and saving seeds, and I heartily applaud these efforts. Yet fewer are willing to devote an hour a day to inner work by engaging in soul-deepening practices.

For many, the Covid pandemic and seemingly endless months of lockdown spurred them to devote time to inner work. Countless stories of the emotional and spiritual benefits of quarantine have been told, accompanied by details of how individuals were profoundly altered by decreased noise, increased alone time and contemplation, and calm, spacious engagement with family in the home. One of those stories will be told in Chapter 11 below.

Nevertheless, the pandemic was traumatizing. None of us has escaped its myriad impacts. Given this reality, I can only wonder how most human beings in industrial cultures intend to navigate climate catastrophe and the likely collapse of their systems without the practice of deep contemplation and reflection.

Likewise, the pandemic motivated many to offer gifts of service to the community—volunteering in food banks, assisting healthcare workers, shopping for neighbors, being a health screener in clinics or hospitals, volunteering to man mental health hotlines, and more. While contemplation and reflection are essential, so is our willingness to serve the human and more-than-human world.

As the unraveling of industrial civilization becomes more traumatic, mental illness will proliferate and become increasingly severe, and without psycho-spiritual stability and mutual support for one another, living fiercely will become untenable, even unimaginable.

In summary, *the more people commit to inner work and service in the world, the less terrified of our predicament they are likely to be.*

Activist and spiritual teacher Richard Rohr, founder of the

Center for Action and Contemplation, writes that, "We need both compassionate action *and* contemplative practice for the spiritual journey. Without action, our spirituality becomes lifeless and bears no authentic fruit. Without contemplation, all our doing comes from ego, even if it looks selfless, and it can cause more harm than good...It doesn't matter which comes first; action may lead you to contemplation, and contemplation may lead you to action."[4]

Please approach this book as a survival manual rather than a repository of new information that you need to read only once and then "move on." Move on to what, I must ask? For unless we learn to live *into* our predicament fiercely, we will be paralyzed and pulverized, and we will assuredly not be undaunted.

Carolyn Baker
Boulder, Colorado, 2022

PART ONE

ENGAGING WITH RAW, EXISTENTIAL REALITIES

Perhaps it was because we were so sociopathically good at collating bad news into a sickening evolving sense of what constituted "normal," or because we looked outside and things seemed still okay. Because we were bored with writing, or reading, the same story again and again, because climate was so global and therefore nontribal it suggested only the corniest politics, because we didn't yet appreciate how fully it would ravage our lives, and because, selfishly, we didn't mind destroying the planet for others living elsewhere on it or those not yet born who would inherit it from us, outraged.

—David Wallace Wells, *The Uninhabitable Earth: Life After Warming* [1]

Before anything different can happen, before people can sense, hear, relate, and imagine differently, there must be a clearing, a decluttering, an initiation into the unknowable; and a letting go of the desires for certainty, authority, hier-

archy, and of insatiable consumption as a mode of relating to everything. We will need a genuine severance that will shatter all projections, anticipations, hopes, and expectations in order to find something we lost about ourselves, about time/space, about the depth of the shit we are in, about the medicines/poisons we carry. This is about pain, about death, about finding a compass, an antidote to separability. This is about being ready to go—to befriend death—before we are ready to return home and to live as grown-ups. [2]

—Vanessa Machado de Oliveira, *Hospicing Modernity: Facing Humanity's Wrongs and the Implications for Social Activism*

CHAPTER 1

EMOTIONS AS ALLIES, NOT ENEMIES

We don't go into a state of shock when something big and bad happens; it has to be something big and bad that we do not yet understand. A state of shock is what results when a gap opens up between events and our initial ability to explain them. When we find ourselves in that position, without a story, without our moorings, a great many people become vulnerable to authority figures telling us to fear one another and relinquish our rights for the greater good. —Naomi Klein[1]

P erhaps nothing more aptly describes the human condition in the second decade of the twenty-first century than "a state of shock that we do not yet understand." We lived through a terrorist attack that rattled the globe in 2001. We survived conflagrations in the Middle East, worldwide recessions, and numerous subsequent terrorist attacks in a variety of countries, and currently we have been living through a global pandemic—all of which have been dreadful and disquieting. Yet none of these tragedies has prepared us for the reality that our planet is dying and that

3

our own species may become extinct. Most humans cannot fully comprehend the implications or ultimate consequences of that statement. For this reason, few members of our species allow themselves to delve deeply into the reality of a terminally ill planet. In fact, we are tragically ill-equipped to do so.

When members of industrially developed cultures encounter such bad news, their first impulse is to fix it, and when they encounter a problem that has no solution, they almost always deny or minimize it. Nothing has prepared the civilized psyche for a *planetary predicament*: a problem that has no solution and which can only be responded to. We may learn how to live with cancer or without a spouse, but few of us can imagine the death of the natural environment and the ruin of the very air we breathe.

Scientists and ecologists studying the demise of our planet invite us to learn how to live resiliently, yet few of us comprehend the word. What does it really mean? To "bounce back," to adapt, to grin and bear it, to never give up, to become a survivalist?

In recent years one of my colleagues defined resilience as *the life-giving ability to shift from a reaction of denial or despair to learning, growing, and thriving in the midst of challenge.* Since then, I have cherished and utilized this definition countless times, as I am doing here.

However, before I deploy this definition in real life, I want to begin by exploring the state of shock—and its concomitant emotions—that is our natural response to incomprehensible devastation. Our planetary predicament demands *emotional* resilience—a skill more challenging than mere emotional *intelligence,* because, while useful, intelligence does not guarantee resilience.

The post-modern, rational mind says that if I know about emotions, I can "manage" them, and all will be well. A mind committed to resilience recognizes how painfully limited "knowing" and "managing" are in a time of unraveling. To appreciate the full impact of our planetary predicament, we must acknowledge that climate chaos is inexorably generating the disintegration of systems such as food, water, electricity, healthcare, law enforcement, education, media, finance, and more, rendering our most heroic attempts to "know" and "manage" patently absurd.

As stated above, this book does not begin with or emphasize climate science, that is, "the facts" of our predicament. At this late date, we know them only too well. After writing about and researching these topics for more than fifteen years and witnessing their ubiquity in the common climate discourse, I doubt that the reader requires more evidence of sea level rise, Arctic ice melt, extreme weather, the imminent death of oceans, respiratory illnesses caused by air pollution, the proliferation of pandemics, species extinction, or soil degradation. In my experience, what the reader urgently craves is guidance for navigating the minefield of emotions that this tsunami of horrors evokes.

To those less familiar with honoring and working with emotions, I invite you to consider that your sanity and possibly your survival in the days ahead may depend on developing your emotional resilience, and the first step in doing so is to recognize that emotions are allies, not enemies. In fact, emotional resilience is an essential part of one's mooring in a sea of emotional, as well as environmental, unraveling. Discounting human emotion because we perceived it as the enemy is precisely why our planet has received a terminal diagnosis. After all, those "frivolous" emotions which sensitize our conscience do not allow us to eviscerate and slaughter innocent animals to embellish our dinner table; they don't allow us to carry on at least four decades of rapacious, implacable oil drilling in the name of the combustion engine; they don't permit us to drive 99% of the four billion species that have evolved on Earth into extinction. Only hyper-rational, emotionally numbed, gluttonous voracity can do that.

Befriending emotions is not the endgame in living fiercely into our predicament, but it is, I believe, the most sane and sensible beginning. Without them we are reluctant to mine the *meaning* in our impasse, and this book asserts that no task is more urgent than doing so. If our planet exists with a terminal diagnosis, our species does as well, even if humanity endures for another million years. But it is more likely that life on Earth has entered a hospice situation—and for many humans, hospice is where they paradoxically encounter, find, or make meaning.

But does meaning really matter?

In every crisis that human beings have ever navigated, many of them have sought to find meaning in adversity. From the Greek philosophers to survivors of the Black Death in medieval Europe to survivors of world wars and those who survived the holocaust, humans appear to be meaning-making creatures.

Author and coach Richard Leider asserts, as I will throughout this book, that nothing matters more.

> Meaning matters. The search for meaning is basic to us all. However, we often examine it only when some crisis forces us to confront it—an arrest, an illness, a death, a divorce, or a loss of job. We take life for granted until a crisis wakes us up and forces us to ask the big questions. Crisis is a catalyst for purpose moments.[2]

Holocaust survivor Viktor Frankl asserted that, "What man actually needs is not a tensionless state, but rather the striving and struggling for some goal worthy of him. What he needs is not the discharge of tension at any cost, but the call of a potential meaning waiting to be fulfilled by him."[3]

Buddhist teacher Judy Lief, writes that:

The fact is that anxiety is an ineffective way of dealing with life's uncertainties and harshness. We should be anxious, up to a point. If we didn't worry about the possibility of very real disasters, that would be stupid. But once something has got our attention, our anxiety gets in the way. It doesn't help us find ways to prevent such disasters, and it doesn't help us figure out how to deal with matters we cannot fix. The Indian master Shantideva advised a clean and simple approach: If you face a problem you can do something about, do it. Why worry? And if there is nothing you can do about it, so be it. Why worry? Emotions like anxiety have two sides. They are messengers—they have something to teach us— but they quickly gather strength and take us over, and we lose it.[4]

If we allow any emotion to consume us, then it is not an ally. Living fiercely into climate meltdown is an emotional and spiritual practice requiring us to fine-tune our relationship with emotions, utilizing them skillfully rather than being engulfed by them.

Buddhist author and activist Joanna Macy, invites us to view the climate crisis as an "invitation to spiritual practice." Margaret Wheatley, leadership coach and management consultant, invites us to become "warriors of the human spirit" with a focus on *who we want to be* amid climate chaos and *what is ours to do* in terms of service to all living beings. From this perspective, a crisis is a terrible thing to waste.

"Purpose moments" amid climate chaos are far more

accessible to us if we experience our emotions as allies that serve to release us from ceaseless intellectualizing and "fighting" nature's consequences. Even as we tirelessly work to mitigate climate devastation, we must embrace our fear, anger, and grief as messengers of meaning. They in themselves are not the meaning we crave, but without their provocation and our attending to them, meaning will forever elude us.

FIERCE PRACTICES

Fierce practices are included at the end of every chapter in this book. They are more effective when we make time to journal and quietly reflect on them without interruption.

- How have I been educated away from experiencing emotions?
- What would being emotionally resilient look like for me?
- What emotions come up for me when I think about being in a state of "planetary hospice"?
- What is an example of a "purpose moment" that I have experienced because of a crisis?

CHAPTER 2

THE FOLLY OF FEARLESSNESS

Fear is a natural reaction to moving closer to the truth. —Pema Chodron[1]

At each turning point in life, we must face our deepest fears in order to grow. —Michael Meade[2]

I began this book in December 2021 when daily high temperatures along the Front Range of Colorado were hovering in the seventies. There was absolutely no precipitation to alleviate the drought this region was already experiencing. Not only was I longing for a change of seasons, but I could not erase the fear of what the summer of 2022 would hold for the entire Western United States. Although I had for years been practicing "living in the present moment," the fear lingered like a nagging laser in my consciousness, alongside the reality that all of this was beyond my control and that fire, drought, and relocation could be inescapable realities in my future.

But I would not have to wait for the summer of 2022. On

December 30, 2021, raging, vehement winds from the west ignited a fire that destroyed over 1,000 homes in the southeastern corner of my county. Starting from that moment, a fire "season" no longer existed in Colorado. I am grateful that I was not personally affected by a wildfire, but I have no illusion that I never will be.

Those of us who have not turned a blind eye to the undeniable facts regarding climate chaos know the danger that every species on Earth is facing. Everyone reading these words who has been willing to engage with the facts has felt the fear of not knowing when, how, or where climate change will upend and possibly destroy our lives. We live our daily routines, engage with family, friends, co-workers, and complete strangers about countless other matters, yet the likelihood that climate catastrophe might *end*, as well as *upend* our lives and the lives of our loved ones, never completely vanishes from our consciousness.

How can we not fear what we know? Why do so many people around us, who unconsciously know what we know, refuse to know consciously?

OUR NEW BOTH/AND WORLD

Everyone reading this book has very likely grown up in a binary culture. From that perspective, two opposing realities cannot be true at the same time, and if someone asks us to live with the paradox, we naively assume we have encountered an exacting Zen master. And yet, paradox is one of the most fundamental realities of human existence. As Carl Jung stated, "Only the paradox comes anywhere near to comprehending the fullness of life."[3]

Climate chaos is real, and it's coming for us. How can we live as if it isn't? We can eat, drink, work, play, or alter our moods in myriad ways, but the fear never goes away. Torna-does and fires in December in the Northern Hemisphere and the eruption of yet another new Covid variant are grim reminders.

Most humans attempt to anesthetize the fear in one way or other, hell-bent on pushing it away or distracting themselves from what they consciously or unconsciously know is inevitable. Others indulge the fear and incessantly pontificate or write from a place of fear within themselves about how stupid everyone else is for not seeing what they see.

Fewer of us are committed to a daily practice of holding the tension of opposites—a perspective offered by Carl Jung and those who embrace Buddhism and other spiritual traditions. In that practice we struggle—and it *is* a struggle—to acknowl-edge our fear, take specific action regarding climate chaos, engage in relationships, work, and creativity, and even main-tain intentional contact with nature. We may at times feel schizophrenic as we bask in the glorious beauty of an epic sunset while realizing that Arctic ice melt has now passed the point of no return, and in fact, is proceeding at a speed that mystifies even the most astute climate scientists.

When we hold the tension of opposites, we do not become paralyzed or debilitated by our fear, nor does it drive us to shame others for their insistence on living in denial. Indeed, we feel more vulnerable. Yet that very vulnerability offers us an opportunity to share our fear with trusted allies in our lives. If we have those allies, we possess an inestimable gift. If we do not have such allies, it is our responsibility to find them.

Moreover, according to Jung, when we are able to hold the tension of opposites, a third option or third way of perceiving the dilemma emerges. Without that tension, we would have remained entrenched in a binary perception of our options.

Two weeks following the Colorado fires mentioned above,

members of a mental health support group in a local church discussed the long-term emotional impacts of the fires. Among the residual effects of the disaster that group members verbalized were:

- Fear for our own safety, for our friends and neighbors, and for pets and wildlife
- Feeling out of control and powerless
- A sense of disbelief and unreality that felt surreal
- Relief that it was over—and guilt for feeling relieved
- Survivor guilt
- Helplessness
- Feeling fragile under the weight of all the losses in one's life, especially hard for the aged
- Grief, sadness, despair, depression
- Gratitude for those who helped me and others
- Feeling more connected to my community because of how we pulled together
- Resigned to catastrophes like urban wildfires as the "new normal"; anger at our complacency and acceptance of climate change
- Apprehension—this is just the beginning of local climate disasters
- Isolation; disconnection from what's happening out there to others
- Anxiety, PTSD—for example how I felt on the next windy day
- Compassion for those who lost everything
- A desire/impulse/need to help others and to be clear about my motivations
- Appreciation for what really matters in my life, especially family, friends, and community.

While owning and discussing their fears and their gratitude did not and will not alter external events, members of the support group reported that being able to do so helped them feel more emotionally resilient and less isolated.

It is only by facing our fear that we develop the courage to persevere. Courage is not developed by sheer will power. It evolves within us, paradoxically, as we become familiar with our vulnerability. It cultivates our values and a robust sense of meaning and purpose.

FIERCE PRACTICES

These practices are more effective when we make time to journal and quietly reflect on them without interruption.

- As I think about climate chaos, what fears do I hold?
- Take at least fifteen minutes to sit quietly and feel your fears about climate chaos. Notice the sensations in your body. Your impulse may be to stop feeling or to start thinking about what action to take in response. Instead, breathe deeply, then notice your fears again and how they show up in your body. Now bring into your consciousness a pleasant or supportive memory of something or someone that comforts you. Notice the sensations in your body with that memory. Breathe into those sensations and deeply feel them. Now take your awareness back to your fears and notice them again. Now, like a swinging pendulum, take your awareness back to the pleasant or supportive memory. Again, like a pendulum, allow your awareness to slowly go back and forth from the fear

to the supportive memory. Notice all the sensations in your body as you do this.

- Do you have an emotionally safe place to discuss your fears of climate chaos? If not, have you considered creating one?

CHAPTER 3

BACKSTROKING IN THE RAGING RIVERS OF GRIEF

Bringing grief and death out of the shadows is our spiritual responsibility, our sacred duty. —Francis Weller, The Wild Edge of Sorrow[1]

Grief is not a feeling; it is a capacity. It is not something that disables you; we are not on the receiving end of grief, we are on the practicing end of grief... Grief is the midwife of your capacity to be immensely grateful for being born. —Stephen Jenkinson, Die Wise: A Manifesto for Sanity and Soul[2]

On countless occasions I have encountered climate activists who are enraged with other members of their species. They carry their bitterness like a prickly-pear cactus shield around them, and while they may be fascinating, intelligent, playful human beings, a part of them holds caustic, corrosive contempt for humanity. Often, they claim to have done more research than most on climate chaos, and they hold their knowledge in hand like a grenade that can decimate anyone who dares to mention that dreaded word "hope." Whatever the currently reported outcomes of climate change, their forecast is irrevocably and predictably *more* dire and catastrophic. As one of these individuals said to me when I first reported on the initial appearance of the Covid-19 virus: "This is nothing. You can't even begin to imagine how fucked we are."

While I cringe when I hear the rantings of individuals who wear their catastrophizing rage toward other humans on their sleeve, I deeply empathize with them because they are being marinated in grief without acknowledging that reality. Whether we own it or not, we are all swirling in rivers of climate grief, whether we are raging, or conversely, when we feel as if we are drowning in grief, or ironically, are so disconnected with our emotions that we don't even feel the wetness of the river.

In this book I am asserting that whatever our response to climate chaos, it is the feeling of grief that we are least familiar with and most in need of. Beneath all of the emotions and thoughts we have about climate meltdown lies a river of sorrow that leads to an ocean of grief.

Our climate grief is connected with all the other forms of grief we are holding, in fact, climate grief is likely to trigger those other forms. We fear climate grief. We are afraid it will stir up all the other forms of grief, overwhelming us, so we deny or distract ourselves with rage and blame.

Nevertheless, if we allow it, our anger can actually take us into the waters of grief. However, those of the so-called spiritual ilk who pontificate about how anger is negative and should be "risen above" sometimes claim that they are channeling Kali (Hindu Goddess, benevolent destroyer) or other symbolic Gods when they express it.

In reality, anger is yet another human emotion like fear or sadness and is no better or worse than any other emotion.

Jeff Brown, author of *Grounded Spirituality*, champions anger expressed but contained, so that we are not harming living beings:

> In fact, anger is a beautiful and bountiful river. It wants to be released into the vaster ocean. It wants to move naturally. When we repress it with premature forgiveness, block it with false positivity, repress it in the name of pseudo-peace, project it onto angry Gods and Goddesses, we just dam our natural flow. The river then turns inward, against the self, or explodes outwardly, against innocents. Better we express it when it is in our awareness—not in a way that is destructive to humanity, but in a way that is authentic and that restores the integrity of our being. Anger isn't the enemy. Misplaced and misidentified anger is. You're not channeling Kali when you express your anger. You are expressing YOURSELF. It's essential that you own that, in order to see the healing all the way through to completion. Let the river flow...[3]

We have a choice to make: Whether we are enraged at humanity or are so much in denial of climate chaos that we consciously feel nothing about it, it is impossible to escape climate grief. We can continue in our attempts to ward it off, or we can allow the waters of grief to seep in. I'm not suggesting a deep dive, but I am encouraging us to start getting wet if we haven't already.

At the same time, I do not wish to shame people who feel angry about human-caused climate change. I feel this anger whenever I read stories about how major fossil fuel and auto manufacturers have known for at least four decades the extent to which they were devastating ecosystems even as they were gorging on economic profits. We *should* feel outraged—their deception is unconscionable. However, while immersing ourselves deeply in rage may lead to impassioned climate activism, it does not catalyze the profound transformation of our souls or our rebirth as individuals. It doesn't touch our core the way that conscious grieving does. What is more, consider that the Earth community may even invite and welcome our grief.

I'M AFRAID I'LL CRY—A CONVERSATION AT THE GYM

At the end of my morning workout, while washing my hands in the women's locker room, a woman asked everyone if they had recently been to Costco, situated as it is on the edge of the remains of the recent Boulder wildfire. I said that I had not been but was planning to go soon. The woman immediately replied,

"You're brave. I haven't gone out there yet. I'm afraid I'll cry."

I replied, "Yes, you probably will."

To which she answered, "But isn't that why we come here? To forget all that?"

I said, "Well, I come here to improve my physical and mental health. It helps me be more perceptive."

She laughed and said, "Fuck being perceptive," and nervously wished me a nice day as she bolted out of the door.

Indigenous cultures skilled in grieving cannot relate to "I'm afraid I'll cry." Here is an example. Francis Weller visited the village of the late Malidoma Somé in Burkina Faso following a grief ritual. He encountered a woman who was smiling radiantly and asked her if she attended the ritual. She replied that she had. Francis commented on her radiant smile, to which she responded, "I'm so happy because I cry all the time."

When we cultivate a conscious relationship with grief, it is no longer an emotion to fear. Not only do we feel better in the short term, but our long-term capacity to fully experience and savor joy is deepened.

However, it is not wise to commit to grieving until we have the support we need. As mentioned above, it is our responsibility to create that support because we probably have no idea now how much we will need it in the future. I have been offering such support for many years alongside others such as Francis Weller,[4] David Kessler,[5] and the Good Grief Network[6] —all resources which can be found online.

Whatever support systems you encounter or create, you are likely to discover that grief offers an invitation to become its apprentice. It asks you to "sign up" to be its student. Doing so does not consign you to a life of sorrow or depression. In fact, in becoming an "apprentice of sorrow,"[7] you are likely to experience (again paradoxically) more aliveness and more joy than are possible in a state of denial or numbness or rage regarding climate chaos.

We do not enter the waters of grief simply because we need to cool off, but because they have somewhere to take us. As sorrow's apprentices, we are given the opportunity to be infused with the indigenous, eco-spiritual consciousness that connects us with all that is alive.

Francis Weller notes:

Grief requires two things to really be moved. One is containment and one is release. If I'm doing it privately, I'm asked to do two jobs at once, which I cannot do, so I end up becoming an ongoing containment vessel for grief but never really allowed to set it down. The community is the containment, a friend is the containment that allows me to then simply do one job, which is to release it, to set it down, to move into it and to express it. But we can't do it in private. We have to remember that grief has always been a communal process; it has always, always, always been communal. Only until the very recent time has it become this very interior, private thing that we're asked to carry alone... with a quality of shame attached to it. Like, why aren't you over that? Or, what's wrong with you? You shouldn't be feeling this. So, what I've noticed over the years is that when we have an emotional experience that is not held by others and given that containment, it begins to have an attachment to it that's based on fear and shame. So I rarely see someone having a pure grief experience; they're having a grief-terror experience or a grief-shame experience, because those other things have become so enmeshed in it. And part of our job as a community when we gather is to begin to take off the fear and take off the shame and simply sit with the sorrows that are around us all the time.[8]

Likewise, when we feel angry about climate chaos, we are having a grief-anger experience. We may feel consumed with the fire of anger in the moment, but in other regions of the psyche, the waters of grief flow, and they long to be experienced and expressed because they have the potential to temper the fire and transport us into deeper layers of our humanity.

CLIMATE GRIEF

Ten years ago, if a client presented a psychotherapist with the idea of "climate grief," the therapist might have perceived the notion as an aspect of the client's pathology or childhood trauma. Today's climate grief landscape is different. The American Psychological Association is now recognizing the reality of climate grief and validating it with clients.[9] The February 2022 *New York Times* article, *When Climate Change Enters the Therapy*

Room, validated countless clients who have sought therapy or support around climate grief, and at the same time, it gave permission to even more individuals to do the same.[10]

I ask: If we are *not* experiencing climate grief, what is *not* happening in the psyche? Obviously, we are not recognizing the severity of our predicament, or if we are, something is preventing us from mourning it.

What is more, becoming an apprentice of sorrow paradoxically offers a kind of "rest" in our commitment to face our predicament while allowing us to do what we can to mitigate it. I am reminded of the exhausted swimmer who occasionally relies on the backstroke to ease their fatigue. Floating on one's back and then stroking makes it easier to breathe and allows the swimmer a reprieve from the intensity of the forward-stroke rhythm. In that sense, conscious grieving provides both release and respite in our awakened responses to climate chaos.

Enormous emphasis in typical climate activism is placed on the "struggle." Dire climate science revelations are often framed as evils that we must "fight." For this reason, I prefer the word "predicament," because without letting anyone off the hook, it reveals that fighting climate chaos is not useful, while skillfully responding to it is. Climate chaos is not a problem to be solved or fought, but a predicament that we can only respond to.

THE SKILL OF GRIEVING

An apprentice is someone who has consented to learn a skill, and apprentices of sorrow commit to learning the skill of grieving. They learn not to resist but rather to open up to the grieving process, not only in terms of the loss of ecosystems but in *every* context of loss.

And how is this useful, you may ask?

It is useful because grieving changes the griever. It compels us to confront the root cause of our predicament: *Estrangement from the embodied experience of intimate connection with all of life, with other humans, and with ourselves.* While we work to minimize the impact of climate chaos on our planet, we commit to maximizing a radically old/new paradigm of being human.

As will often be emphasized in this book, the existential crisis of climate chaos demands that we confront life, death, and meaning in a plethora of contexts and forms in order to become not only apprentices of sorrow, but humble students of the Earth community.

With the caring support of others who are grieving the loss of our planet, we allow ourselves to grieve and in doing so, allow our magnificent and beloved ecosystems to reveal more fully who they are and who we are. It appears that humanity had become incapable of appreciating and honoring this relationship until the very demise of Earth could no longer be denied. The climate crisis now comes to us as a shattering epiphany, but also as a potential inflection point in the evolution of human consciousness. Grief may offer a golden gateway on that journey, for as Francis Weller writes:

We were not meant to live shallow lives, pocked by meaningless routines and the secondary satisfactions of happy hour. We are the inheritors of an amazing lineage, rippling with memories of life lived intimately with bison and gazelle, raven and the night sky. We are designed to encounter this life with amazement and wonder, not resignation and endurance. *This is at the very heart of our grief and sorrow.* The dream of full-throated living, woven into our very being, has often been forgotten and neglected, replaced by a societal fiction of productivity and material gain. No wonder we seek distractions. Every sorrow we carry extends from the absence of what we require to stay engaged in this "one wild and precious life." And every sorrow is made more difficult to metabolize by that absence. Grief work offers us a trail leading back to the vitality that is our birthright. When we fully honor our many losses, our lives become more fully able to embody the wild joy that aches to leap from our hearts into the shimmering world.[11]

FIERCE PRACTICES

These practices are more effective when we make time to journal and quietly reflect on them without interruption.

- Take time to make a list of your losses. I suggest beginning with early childhood. What did you not have that you needed? Who were the people that were there for you and that were not? Reflect on your life from that time, asking these same questions: *What did I lose? Who was there for me in the losses? What are some of the losses I have not grieved?*
- What are my sorrows about our global predicament? What hurts my heart the most?
- When I grieve or think about grieving, what shaming messages come to mind?
- Who can I talk with about my grief?
- If you are comfortable with grieving, make a list of the gifts you have received from it.

CHAPTER 4
TITRATING WOKENESS

The essence of 'woke' is awareness. What you are newly aware of (a pay gap, systemic racism, unchecked privilege) and what to do with that newfound knowledge is the question. And the answer keeps changing depending on who you talk to. But regardless, you've answered the wakeup call, pushed your way out of bed and are now listening. —Kenya Hunt[1]

Being woke is not about being right, saying "down with the man" or winning an argument. It's about accurately understanding someone's experience and embracing paradigm shifts for the global progression of people. —Raven Cras, New Yorker, author, poet, activist[2]

Most readers of this book want to be "woke." In fact, it is not possible to be "undaunted" without being aware, and it is certainly impossible to live fiercely into our global predicament in a state of denial or delusion. Yet if we are to honor our emotions, our psyches, and our bodies, we must lovingly care for ourselves enough to avoid overwhelm. The word *titrate* was originally used in the field of chemical research: "Titration, a process of chemical analysis in which the quantity of some constituent of a sample is determined by adding to the measured sample an exactly known quantity of another substance with which the desired constituent reacts in a definite, known proportion."[3]

In chemistry, titration refers to the amount of concentration of a particular chemical that is in play. Titration or titrating in the psychological realm simply means regulating the amount of information or the quality of information one is ingesting. While it is necessary and valuable to be woke, it is equally necessary not to become overwhelmed.

Denial is a defense mechanism that serves to prevent overwhelm. When we do not have the internal or external resources to prevent overwhelm, we unconsciously resort to—or remain in—denial. When we judge others for "being in denial," we are probably forgetting about our own experiences of not wanting to know about things which we feel powerless to change or which carry such an emotional charge for us that at some point in our lives, we needed to deny them.

Most of humanity is in denial about the severity of our predicament because to fully acknowledge the severity would prove overwhelming. Thus, humans deny or minimize the dire reality of climate chaos and its likely outcome. So yes, the woman at the gym I mentioned earlier, who was fearful of seeing the ashes from the wildfire and said, "Fuck being perceptive," is exemplary. If you are tempted to scoff at her, look into your own heart. Few among us choose to contemplate their own death, and even fewer choose to contemplate the death of their descendants. Conversely, I have known individuals who chose to isolate themselves for an entire week because they were determined to learn everything possible about climate chaos in that amount of time, but those brave souls are rare. Many of us are willing to take a peek at the very bad news for a few minutes, perhaps even an hour, then pull the covers over our heads as soon as possible.

For many years I have worked with individuals who come to me in a state of overwhelm or panic who either feel shattered by learning about our predicament or feel compelled to act impulsively to attempt to escape it. These are natural reactions to ingesting too much information too quickly and not titrating it. However, no one tells us directly that the realities revealed by climate science are so dire that we are likely to feel overwhelmed if we actually examine them. Many people feel overwhelmed from simply seeing or hearing a headline about climate change.

Which is yet another reason I chose to write this book. In fact, everything we do in response to climate chaos is a choice. We can choose to stop learning anything about it and commit to a path of denial and obliviousness. Who could blame us? I believe that no one should be judged for making that choice. If you have a terminal illness, you have every right to do nothing about it. However, you are probably not the only one affected by that choice, and then the real question becomes: How do I live with this information, face climate chaos full-on, do so in relationship with other human beings, and still not become overwhelmed?

The next question then immediately presents itself: How do I respond to our global predicament? What actions do I choose to take to mitigate it? At this point, can it even *be* mitigated?

Another question arises: Who do I choose to be, and how do I choose to live in the face of the facts that I have allowed myself to learn? This question, however, should precede the last one.

As this book will reveal, your life going forward from this

moment will be all about *being* and *doing*, unless you choose to go back to sleep.

If you choose to stay awake and aware, you need to titrate your wokeness. The following practices may be helpful.

FIERCE PRACTICES

These practices are more effective when we make time to journal and quietly reflect on them without interruption.

Take time to reflect on the following:

- When did you begin waking up to our human and ecological predicament?
- What were the first emotions you felt when you began to wake up?
- Do you sometimes feel overwhelmed? When you feel overwhelmed, how do you respond?
- What are the emotional and physical signals that let you know you are getting overwhelmed?
- Titrating wokeness is about increasing your knowledge about our predicament, but simultaneously alternating it with enjoying nature, appreciating beauty, practicing self-care, and enjoying life. How do you titrate your wokeness?
- Who are your allies? Who can you safely speak with about your concerns related to our predicament?

CHAPTER 5

THEY DON'T SEE WHAT I SEE

Any viable worldview must contain many worldviews, and it must arise from within us and between us... What is called for is the capacity to find and support the growing movement of people who think and feel across frames and contexts at scale—a process that entails an encounter with the nature, meaning, and purpose of life. —Jonathan Rowson, Director of *Perspectiva*[1]

Would you rather be correct, or would you prefer to be connected? —Richard Rohr[2]

One of the reasons I write books is that for me, books are not merely instruments of information distribution, but often present opportunities for readers to speak their truth, their pain, their fears—and their gratitude for being validated. If a book stimulates the reader at all, they usually want to discuss some aspects of it and ask questions of other readers.

No sooner did I begin writing books about climate chaos and the collapse of systems than people began approaching me for life coaching and inviting me to present workshops and retreats. The rewards of answering those invitations have been inestimable to me personally and to countless individuals with whom I have worked.

Often our conversations began (and still begin) with, "But I don't have anyone to talk to about these subjects because almost no one sees what I see."

As I question people about why this is so challenging for them, I often discover that the deeper issue is a not only a feeling of being alone with what they know, but also a sense of isolation, estrangement, and feeling perceived as extreme, pessimistic, depressed, or even crazy. It's as if needing others to see what they see begins to define their lives. Thus, I find myself puzzled about why the discussion of our global predicament is so monumentally important to some individuals. I understand that we all feel more comfortable when others see what we see. But why is it not merely a matter of comfort for some, but almost a matter of life and death? I assure you, I am not being hyperbolic about this.

If one has been diagnosed with a terminal illness, the terrible news is less agonizing if one can talk with others who have the same illness. Experiences of empathy, support, and camaraderie are often the best medicine. Similarly, if we consider the possibility that our species has been diagnosed with extinction, the angst we feel when that possibility is recognized is minimized by dialoging with other humans who get it.

Nevertheless, why is it impossible for some awakened individuals to converse about a plethora of other topics with friends or relatives who don't get it? Why is "they don't see what I see" so seemingly impossible for some people to accept?

Many individuals believe that they can never have meaningful, emotional intimacy with others who do not see what they see. It's as if the inability to converse about their mutual death sentence precludes the possibility of moments of emotional and spiritual depth in their engagement with others.

People often say, "Well I can't just talk about the weather with my relatives!" To which I often reply, "I suppose it depends on *how* you talk about the weather. They want to talk about the local forecast, and you want to talk about climate catastrophe."

But what would happen if we did just "talk about the weather" with those who don't see what we see?

Western civilization has shaped us to be such myopic, purpose-driven, solution-focused, creatures that it is often incredibly challenging to just be present with another human being whether we are discussing the local weather forecast or the extinction of species. When we silently or verbally *demand* that another individual see what we see, we are actually not relating to them at all. In fact, the relationship subtly centers around *me* and *my* fears, *me* and *my* sense of powerlessness to change the future. In fact, is authentic dialog even possible as long as I demand that you see what I see? In other words, I need to *feel* my fears—fears for myself, fears for you, fears for the ecosystems. I need to do the inner work that climate catastrophe confronts me with, even if I have no one to discuss it with. And if I am afraid for the future of someone else, I need to feel my fear for them and also allow myself to be temporarily incapacitated by the grief I feel for myself, for my friends and relatives, for the trees, the animals, the oceans, the rivers, the forests, and for every living being on Earth. All of this is heartbreaking and points to the estrangement we feel from our human and more than human relatives.

Anna Freud introduced the concept of defense mechanisms —the natural processes in the human psyche by which we defend against information that could harm or overwhelm us.[3] One of those is denial. Quite naturally, most humans do not want to hear about or discuss climate chaos. The more perilous it appears to be, the more we tend to avoid the topic. It is profoundly distressing, even terrifying. Thus, we develop what Michael Dowd describes as "adaptive inattention." More specifically, Stephen Jenkinson writes:

> Inattention to the world's ecological state is well-advised because attention to it mitigates against your happiness, your contentment, and your sense of wellbeing...Having a conscience now is a grief-soaked proposition...Whatever "spiritual awakening" may have meant in past times and places, if you awaken in our time, you awaken with a sob.[4]

Consider that, as a result of our entrapment in the story of separation from the web of life, our very inability to be fully present with another human being as we discuss any subject of climate chaos or as we sit silently together and stare into space, is the precise cause of our planetary predicament. Your father may deny climate change entirely, but have you hung out with him while "talking about the weather" and noticed his facial expressions, his body language, the changes in his voice since you were a kid, the wrinkles on his hands, his ability to sit quietly with you and really notice you, or conversely, his compulsion to laugh nervously as he demonstrates to you how thoroughly uncomfortable he is in his own skin? Have you noticed what it's like for you to be present with people who are truly present with you as opposed to being present with people who have no idea how to be present with you? Have you noticed the emotions you feel in the former situation and the emotions you feel in the latter situation? None of this has anything to do with whether they agree with you about our planetary predicament or whether they see what you see.

The ultimate issue is: *Do we know how to be present with another human being? Do we know how to authentically see them and allow them to authentically see us even when they don't see what we see?*

So instead of blaming or cursing or shaming or shunning people who don't see what we see, how about actually seeing *them*? How about seeing their deep wounds, their vulnerability, their terror of things they don't understand, and the toll that the story of separation has taken on them. They may never become our BFF, but do we have the capacity to look beyond whatever they believe about the future into their deeper humanity?

Consider that climate catastrophe may be asking us to acknowledge that our refusal to see and be seen is both a cause and a symptom of our predicament and that we only worsen our predicament by our adolescent insistence on *agreement as superior to presence.*

We have come to believe that intimacy should feel awesome, but sometimes it doesn't. Sometimes it breaks our hearts or irritates us or rocks our world. What it does mean, however, is that we are present—all of our being is fully there in the moment.

Recently, my friend and colleague Zhiwa Woodbury penned an article entitled, "What If We Are All We've Got?"[5] in which he opined:

What does it mean to be human in the Anthropocene? This is not a question to be answered by academics. Rather, it is the question of our times, one to be taken up and answered by everyone who shares the existential concern over our dilemma. Our answer to this question, as reflected in how we change in responsive ways, will determine our collective fate as a species, as well as the fate of this living planet.

That is the gravity and ultimate significance of the Anthropocene. It's not anthropocentric, as some mistakenly assume. Rather, it means that our actions are shaping the future today. It's a responsibility we cannot shirk.

Distancing other humans who do not see what we see is the direct opposite of what it means to be human in the Anthropocene. *Presence*, not estrangement, is being asked of us because "we are all we've got."

FIERCE PRACTICES

These practices are more effective when we make time to journal and quietly reflect on them without interruption.

- What has been your experience with "seeing what others don't see"?
- How have you responded to people who question the severity of our predicament?
- What are you *not* seeing about them? What might you be missing about their lives?
- Experiment with just "hanging out" with someone who doesn't see what you see. What do you notice about them? Take time to notice their tone of voice, facial expressions, mood, appearance, body language. Do any of these offer a clue about why they don't see what you see?
- Do they have any qualities that you also enjoy? What do you appreciate about them?

CHAPTER 6
DEEP ADAPTATION

The overarching mission of the Deep Adaptation Forum is to embody and enable loving responses to our predicament, so that we reduce suffering while saving more of society and the natural world. —Deep Adaptation Forum[1]

Deep Adaptation is a way of framing our current global situation that can help people to refocus on what's important in life while our social order collapses under the weight of its own consumption, pollution, and inequality. We are finding new ways of being with ourselves and being together, no matter what happens. —Deep Adaptation Forum[2]

In 2018, Jem Bendell, University of Cumbria Professor of Sustainability Leadership, published a paper entitled, "Deep Adaptation: A Map for Navigating Climate Tragedy." In the paper, Bendell shared his own experiences of coming to terms with our predicament and proposed three pivotal responses to it: *Resilience*—the capacity to maintain valued norms and behaviors that societies seek to maintain throughout our predicament; *Relinquishment:* Letting go of the assets, behaviors, and beliefs that could worsen climate tragedy; and *Restoration:* rediscovering attitudes and approaches to life and organization that our hydrocarbon-fueled civilization eroded.[3]

The word "deep" indicates that strong measures are required to adapt to an unraveling of western industrial lifestyles.[4] In other words, the Deep Adaptation (DA) movement argues that we cannot adapt to our predicament unless we fully understand how it unfolded, and unless we examine our role in that process. Introspection is one of the "strong measures" that must occur, superseding a distanced, dispassionate, cerebral accumulation of facts. This necessitates recognizing that emotions are *not* our enemies and that we willingly acknowledge our fear, anger and grief in response to climate tragedy. Such soul-searching is essential if we are to become resilient. We cannot evaluate what norms and behaviors we wish to maintain in the face of climate and societal collapse solely by means of the intellect. Fortunately, our introspection need not and must not take place in isolation. It demands communal as well as personal reflection.

Naked introspection then informs what we need to relinquish. At the heart of any process of conscious grieving is the willingness—in fact the necessity—of letting go. What possessions, attitudes, assumptions, and behaviors impair our resilience and encumber us as we work to strengthen it? And how do any of these worsen the climate tragedy?

Although we cannot restore many aspects of climate catastrophe, other facets of the tragedy offer us opportunities to reimagine and literally restore what has been lost, not merely in terms of recuperating material losses, but reimagining new possibilities for utilizing them.

Since Jem Bendell published his original paper, the concept of Deep Adaptation has gone viral, particularly in Europe.

Since then, DA has developed a plethora of courses, work-shops, forums, and local projects for promoting and strengthening the three "R's."

For the past fifteen years I have worked diligently to cultivate and promote the core concepts of DA, far in advance of the release of Jem Bendell's historic paper. Thus, this book is an expression of my commitment to the principles of DA which I believe humanity must now fully embrace and employ.

FIERCE PRACTICES

These practices are more effective when we make time to journal and quietly reflect on them without interruption.

- Read Jem Bendell's "Deep Adaptation" paper and explore the abundant resources available at the Deep Adaptation and Deep Adaptation Forum websites.
- What efforts are you personally making to mitigate the effects of climate chaos in your community?
- How are you and your community strengthening your resilience—that is, your capacity to respond and deeply adapt in the face of climate tragedy?
- As stated above, introspection and reflection are necessary aspects of resilience. What have your experiences of practicing these revealed *to* you and *about* you?
- What have you personally chosen to relinquish in response to our predicament?
- How are you and your community "rediscovering attitudes and approaches to life and organization that our hydrocarbon-fueled civilization eroded"?

CHAPTER 7
UNALTERABLE UNCERTAINTY

In an increasingly complex, unpredictable world, what matters most isn't IQ, willpower, or confidence in what we know, it's how we deal with what we don't understand. —Jamie Holmes, author of *Nonsense: The Power of Not Knowing*[1]

But it's not impermanence per se, or even knowing we're going to die, that is the cause of our suffering, the Buddha taught. Rather, it's our resistance to the fundamental uncertainty of our situation. —Pema Chodron, Buddhist teacher[2]

It's tough to make predictions, especially about the future. —Yogi Berra[3]

Perhaps nothing in Western intellectual discourse is more sacrosanct than certainty. Does one really have a right to speak if they can't document what they say? Furthermore, what are the sources? If one can't verify their statements using reliable sources, then what they speak is likely to be only opinion, not truth. However, as I will address later in this book, we have entered an age when certainty and sources are becoming meaningless in an era of gaslighting and mega-misinformation. Certainty, based on facts, is circling the drain in a world awash in social media and "alternative facts."

While I deplore the decline of critical thinking in Western culture, the loss of certainty, particularly about what the future may hold, may blessedly be compelling humans to acknowledge that certainty has always been a chimera as Jamie Holmes asserts in *Nonsense: The Power of Not Knowing.*[4]

As climate chaos and its attendant collapse of systems intensifies, amid the plethora of moods that will ensue, perhaps nothing will become more ubiquitous than uncertainty. Moreover, it may be that nothing in the likely worst-case scenarios ahead will more brutally drive humans mad than the inability to cope with uncertainty. Yet, the more we demand certainty, the more distressing the unraveling will be. It is therefore imperative that we learn how to dance with, rather than attempt to vanquish uncertainty.

All great world traditions offer wisdom for coping with uncertainty, but perhaps the Buddhist tradition is the most specific and the most strategic in doing so.

The Buddhist poet Jane Hirshfield captures it beautifully in her poem *Against Certainty*:

> *There is something out in the dark that wants to*
> *   correct us.*
> *Each time I think "this," it answers "that."*[5]

Civilized humans are easily seduced by certainty. It is our consummate soporific.

As I write these words, sitting as I am in a winter that isn't winter, I can only imagine (and dread) the summer that lies ahead that is likely to bring blistering temperatures and blazing wildfires. Will I become yet another homeless climate refugee with few or no possessions in a world where disaster assistance and insurance coverage may soon become artifacts of the pre-climate change era? Where will I go? What will I do? Will I even survive?

Yet I continue to write—holding my "plans" lightly, marinated in uncertainty.

HOLDING THE TENSION OF OPPOSITES

Profoundly influenced by indigenous and other wisdom traditions such as Buddhism, Carl Jung, as noted above, introduced Western psychology to the notion of holding the tension of opposites—embracing the "this" and the "that" of which Hirshfield speaks in her poem. Thus, I may become a homeless, impoverished climate refugee or I may have the opportunity to relocate to another location or I may die or I may remain personally untouched by climate catastrophe for some time. Each possibility is a reality to consider and prepare for to the best of my ability. To desperately grasp one option as inevitable is to be seduced by the chimera of certainty. What is being asked of me is to hold the tension of perhaps many scenarios and live my life with that uncertainty.

Francis Weller and I have already invited all of us to become "apprentices of sorrow." Likewise, I invite us to become students of uncertainty. As we live into climate chaos and ultimately, the end of our days, and as we navigate the unprecedented demise of our habitat, we have an opportunity to ponder how to become *students* of our predicament. Students do not just learn, they also act. Moreover, it is equally true that climate chaos and its many layers of unraveling offer an opportunity to become a profoundly transformed human being, even in the final moments of our demise.

In case you hadn't noticed, we are well beyond consideration of how we are going to physically survive climate chaos.
We have entered the force field of the transformation of
consciousness. We have a mandate to become a previously
unimagined species of human—a more *human* human for
whom compassion, kindness, truthfulness, integrity, and
wisdom-warriorhood define us moment to moment.

What is wisdom-warriorhood? Buddhist teacher and leadership consultant Meg Wheatley notes that:

> Warriors only arise at specific times when the current soci-
> ety, ruler, or nation is endangered. Otherwise, there is no
> need for them to shift their priorities to the role of service
> and self-sacrifice, or to train themselves to be of wise service.
>
> Warriors for the human spirit are arising because the
> human spirit needs protection. We are peaceful warriors,
> refraining from using aggression and fear to do our work.
> We recognize the harm being done to people, to the planet,
> and all life. We have identified where we are historically in
> the well-documented pattern of civilization and its fall. We
> know that collapse is here.[6]

In her 2010 contemplative book *Perseverance*, Wheatley
writes about "dwelling in uncertainty." I notice that she is not
suggesting avoiding uncertainty or surviving uncertainty or
moving quickly through it. Rather, she uses the word *dwelling*.
A dweller is someone who has taken residence in a particular
place and embraced it as home. Her use of this word is an invitation to embrace uncertainty as *our* new home. We now live in
constant uncertainty about climate, habitat, health, prosperity,
career, safety, and every level of security to which we are
accustomed. Like sorrow's apprentice, we have also become
our predicament's student. In other words, I accept that this is

my life now. What am I being asked to learn, feel, embrace, heal, resist, and serve? Thus, the entire notion of being an "optimist" or a "pessimist" has become absurd. Or as Wheatley writes:

> Rather than thinking one perspective is preferable to the other, let's notice that both are somewhat dangerous. Either position, optimism or pessimism, keeps us from fully engaging with the complexity of this time. If we see only troubles, or only opportunities, in both cases we are blinded by our need for certainty, our need to know what's going on, to figure things out so we can be useful...
>
> The challenge is to refuse to categorize ourselves. We don't have to take sides or define ourselves as either optimists or pessimists. Much better to dwell in uncertainty, hold the paradoxes, live in the complexities and contradictions without needing them to resolve.[7]

FIERCE PRACTICES

These practices are more effective when we make time to journal and quietly reflect on them without interruption.

- Having read this chapter, what are you feeling? Anxious? Angry? Resistant? Confused? Relieved? Sad?
- What are your concerns about your personal climate future?
- Do you sometimes experience a tendency within yourself to either embrace a pessimistic perspective about our global predicament or conversely, to revert to sheer denial of its seriousness?
- If you tend to gravitate toward a pessimistic, "we're

screwed" perspective, what emotions do you experience with that perspective? If you tend to gravitate toward denial, what emotions do you experience with it? How does either position help you avoid uncertainty?

- What is it like for you to live in uncertainty about anything, but particularly about our planetary predicament?

CHAPTER 8
WHAT MATTERS MOST?

Once man's search for the meaning of life is successful, it not only renders him happy but also gives him the capability to cope with suffering. —Viktor Frankl, *Man's Search for Meaning*[1]

I have never been through a civilization-wide transformation before, and neither have you; we are in uncharted waters together. There is a war taking place in heaven concerning the soul of humanity, and it will be fought in each person's heart, every day, without rest, and into the foreseeable future. I have no choice but to sound metaphysical and religious, because this is where the psyche goes when it enters the liminal. —Zachary Stein, *Covid 19: A War Broke Out in Heaven*[2]

A few moments ago, I watched live footage from one of the towns hardest-hit by the December 2021 torna-does. The carnage was almost unfathomable, raging as it did just weeks before Christmas. People in myriad states of trauma with nothing but the clothing they were wearing spoke of the horrors of the twister, even as they were helping their neighbors sift through the wreckage to find possible survivors and mementos of their vanished lives. Repeatedly, people affirmed that what mattered most to them was not Christmas shopping or holiday plans, but the well-being of their family members and neighbors.

Almost without exception, disaster survivors report that the trauma of loss and tragedy changed them profoundly and compelled them to reflect, amid the horror, upon what matters most. Following his liberation from Auschwitz, Viktor Frankl wrote in his book *Man's Search for Meaning* that, "Those who have a 'why' to live, can bear with almost any 'how'." This chapter dives deeply into the "why" that allows some human beings to survive incomprehensible trauma and shattering physical and psychological wounding.

A fundamental "why" is the human capacity to make meaning of our experiences. In December 2021, as I bore witness to yet another climate-induced tragedy slashing through communities and individual lives, I could only wonder how survivors would be changed and to what extent making meaning of the tragedy would sustain them. A few weeks later, as fire ravaged a portion of my community, the question of how people would be changed was and is being answered in real time.

EUDAIMONIA

Although Abraham Maslow did not include it in his Hierarchy of Needs, the ability to find or create meaning within our experiences is inherent within us, even at the lowest levels of the Hierarchy, because it is so fundamentally who we are. In his book *The Patterning Instinct*, British author Jeremy Lent asserts that "humans are driven by an instinct to pattern meaning into the world."[3] In a more recent work by Lent, *The Web of*

Meaning, he argues that the very essence of our humanity is a quest for meaning and purpose and notes that

"Aristotle made a crucial distinction between two forms of happiness: *Hedonia* and *Eudaimonia.*" *Hedonia,* of course, is a transient state of happiness brought about by pleasurable stimuli whereas *Eudaimonia is a state of satisfaction brought about by fulfilling one's true nature.*[4]

More importantly, attending to our true nature allows us to flourish even in the face of adversity. Related to fulfilling our true nature is the emotion of awe or the sense of being part of or in the presence of something vast and greater than our own limited existence.

Meaning-making is far more than parroting glib slogans like "Everything happens for a reason," or "God moves in mysterious ways." It is the sense that making meaning is not just something I do but is, in fact, part of who I am, and that life is actually asking me to commit to the task, particularly with regard to all of my unwanted and uninvited life experiences.

As I write these words, I'm aware that I would not need to write them for an indigenous person familiar with their tradition because meaning-making is a way of life just as knowing when to plant or harvest or hunt is. Moreover, in the indigenous community, meaning-making is not so much about me and the fulfillment of my personal nature, but the "sacred hoop," of which the Lakota elder Black Elk spoke, that forms an interlocking circle of connectedness with all that is.

In fact, Comanche activist La Donna Harris notes four central values shared by indigenous people around the world that she names *The Four R's:* The first is *Relationship* or kinship not only with family and tribe, but with all of life. Or in the words of the Lakota, "All my relations." The second is *Responsibility:* the community obligation to identify and nurture and care for those relations. *Reciprocity* is balance or flow—the give and take of relationships. *Redistribution* is the obligation to share what one possesses, not necessarily materially, but in terms of skills, time, and energy.[5]

These values do not center around the individual, but rather the community. They echo the African principle of Ubuntu, which literally means, "I am because you are; you are because I am."

African American minister and theologian Reverend Jacqui Lewis writes in her extraordinary book, *Fierce Love*:

> Even before COVID-19 showed up in our global family, we were living in what I call "hot-mess times." In our current context, race and ethnicity, caste and color, gender and sexuality, socioeconomic status and education, religion and political party have all become reasons to divide and be conquered by fear and rancor. . . Put simply, we are in a perilous time, and the answer to the question "Who are we to be?" will have implications for generations to come.
>
> We have a choice to make. We can answer this question with diminished imagination, by closing ranks with our tribe and hiding from our human responsibility to heal the world. Or we can answer the question of who we are to be another way: We can answer it in the spirit of *ubuntu*. The concept comes from the Zulu phrase *Umuntu ngumuntu ngabantu,* which literally means that a person is a person through other people. Another translation is, "I am who I am because we are who we are.". . . With this in mind, *who I will be* is deeply related to *who you are.* In other words, we are each impacted by the circumstances that impact those around us. What hurts you hurts me. What heals you heals me. What causes you joy causes me to rejoice, and what makes you sad also causes me to weep.[6]

INDRA'S NET

Not unlike the sacred hoop of Black Elk is the Jewel Net of Indra from the Buddhist tradition. The story asserts that in the heavenly abode of the god Indra there is a net that stretches infinitely in all directions. In every node of the net hangs a glittering jewel. In fact there are infinite numbers of jewels, all polished so perfectly that if you inspect any one jewel, you will see all other jewels reflected in it. Astonishingly, the reflection process contains infinite dimensions.

Congruent with Indra's Net is the Buddhist concept of the Boddhisatva. He or she has worked tirelessly to attain enlightenment and just as they stand at the threshold of enlightenment, they choose instead to return to the world to help awaken all beings from needless suffering. In this way, the Boddhisatva recognizes their interdependence with all sentient beings and realizes that the notion of a separate self is an illusion.

MYSTICAL EXPERIENCES AND THE PERENNIAL PHILOSOPHY

Throughout all the great traditions of the world, mystical experiences offer further opportunities to experience one's profound interconnectedness with the web of life. Meditation is one avenue for experiencing the mystical, as are prayer, vision questing, pilgrimages, the ingestion of psychedelic substances, ritual, fasting, and more.

Whatever the path, connection with something greater than the rational mind and human ego is an inherent longing within the human psyche. Many argue that "something greater" does not exist while others who prefer to tout their self-sufficiency or their existential angst scoff at the notion—

all of which lend credence to the need for a relationship with something greater. In the absence of that relationship, we tend to be ruled by the human ego, attended by self-will and narcissism.

One characteristic in common with all mystical experiences is a vast sense of oneness and all-encompassing wholeness. They are direct experiences with the sacred. Religion offers its *opinions* about the sacred; mysticism offers sacred *encounters*. An apt analogy might be that religion is like reading a book *about* parenting, whereas parenting is the direct experience of *engaging in* parenting.

Immediately after World War II, Aldous Huxley, a British philosopher and novelist, published his book *The Perennial Philosophy*. The book is essentially an anthology of short passages taken from traditional Eastern texts and the writings of Western mystics, organized by subject and topic, with short connecting commentaries. While we tend to assume that mystics lived only in ancient times, modern mystics include scientists as well as philosophers and theologians, such as Ralph Waldo Emerson as well as the physicist Erwin Schrodinger, who wrote, "Inconceivable as it seems to ordinary reason, you—and all other conscious beings as such—are all in all." And of course, Albert Einstein viewed our sense of separateness as "an optical delusion of consciousness."[7]

In recent years I have come to a new realization and appreciation of perennial wisdom and now view it as a metaphorical river that flows beneath all traditions. One of my favorite literary sources is *The World Wisdom Bible: Perennial Wisdom for the Spiritually Independent*, edited by Rami Shapiro.

MEANING-MAKING REQUIRES CONNECTION

In *The Patterning Instinct*, Jeremy Lent argues that humans have evolved an instinct to pattern meaning into the world to a greater degree—as far as we know—than any other species. He also asserts that, "When we are disconnected from things, when things lose their meaning, we feel bad. When a new pattern comes together, we feel good."[8] What is also true, according to Lent, is that for those reductionists who look for meaning in indivisible particles, it is difficult to make meaning. Western culture focuses on linear, purpose-driven behavior—actions with a beginning, middle and endpoint. However, if we see meaning as arising, like Indra's Net, from an infinite array of interconnections, we recognize that our experiences only contain meaning to the extent that they are connected with other nodes in the web of meaning.[9]

Lent summarizes the crux of meaning-making in his assertion that:

> Each of us can choose to delete those parts of our consciousness that attune to the love and suffering of others, to the sentience of all life on Earth and to the sublime glory of the universe. But that choice inevitably leads to a loss of meaning in life.[10]

The late Buddhist teacher Thich Nhat Hahn coined the term *Interbeing* and encouraged his students to intentionally extend their self-identity to incorporate everything and everyone without exception. "Practice," he said, "until you recognize your presence in everyone else on the bus, in the subway, in the concentration camp, working in the fields, in a leaf, in a caterpillar, in a dew drop, in a ray of sunshine."

In a poignant poem, Thich Nhat Hahn writes:

I am the twelve-year-old girl
Who throws herself into the ocean...
I am the pirate,
My heart is not yet capable
Of seeing and loving...
Please call me by my true names,
So I can hear all of my cries and laughter at
    once,
So I can see that my joy and pain are one.[11]

There, in the mountains of rubble in communities leveled by the December 2021 tornadoes, people struggled to find each other when everything else in their lives was gone. As you read these words, you already know that survivors in countless communities around the world will find themselves struggling to find each other as wave after wave of climate disasters pummel them. The question "Why?" will tearfully reverberate in wrenching anguish from the throats of millions of survivors in the coming years as they bury their dead and attempt to navigate their climate refugee status. If they didn't know before, they will then have laser clarity about what matters most to them.

But I have been speaking in third person, as if I or you will not be among them. Or, as if I or you will physically survive climate catastrophe. Whether or not we do, nothing is more important than committing to cherishing and nurturing the *why* that will carry us through the *how*.

Climate chaos is not merely an ecological tragedy. It is an existential crisis for all life on Earth. It is a matter of life and death—yours and mine. Some have asserted that we are in a state of "planetary hospice" and that we should live accordingly. Those living with a potentially terminal illness cannot avoid issues of meaning and gnawing questions of what matters most. I believe that climate catastrophe is asking us to be fully engaged in meaning-making, regardless of what lies or does not lie ahead. It rudely and abruptly vanishes our rationalist, materialist delusions that life is a meaningless exercise conducted by human organisms operating exclusively in response to electrical impulses in the brain. If we are to adapt to our predicament deeply, then we must begin by attending to our true nature.

FIERCE PRACTICES

These practices are more effective when we make time to journal and quietly reflect on them without interruption.

- What matters most to you, and how does that inform your responses to climate chaos? Take plenty of time to reflect (and write) about this.
- As you consider the word *Eudaimonia*, what do you experience as your true nature? Take plenty of time to contemplate this question.
- What relationships matter most to you? Why? Who have you become? Or, who are you becoming as a result of them?

CHAPTER 9

RECOVERING FROM ADDICTION TO HOPE

Hope is a dimension of the soul...an orientation of the spirit, an orientation of the heart. It transcends the world that is immediately experienced and is anchored somewhere beyond its horizons... It is not the conviction that something will turn out well, but the certainty that something makes sense regardless of how it turns out. —Vaclav Havel[1]

Do not depend on the hope of results...you may have to face the fact that your work will be apparently worthless and even achieve no result at all, if not perhaps results opposite to what you expect. As you get used to this idea, you start more and more to concentrate not on the results, but on the value, the rightness, the truth of the work itself... You gradually struggle less and less for an idea and more and more for specific people... In the end, it is the reality of personal relationship that saves everything. —Thomas Merton[2]

I said to my soul, be still and wait without hope, for hope would be hope for the wrong thing; wait without love, for love would be love

of the wrong thing; there is yet faith, but the faith and the love are
all in the waiting. Wait without thought, for you are not ready for
thought: So the darkness shall be the light, and the stillness the
dancing. —T.S. Eliot, "East Coker"[3]

One of my direct intentions in writing this book is to dismantle all forms of conventional, culturally cherished hope that the reader may have. While that may sound like a brutal admission, I assert that nothing has been more brutal than the murder of this planet in the name of our hope that climate chaos will diminish, deteriorate, or entirely disappear—or that our species will mitigate it sufficiently so that it can be reversed or ended. In fact, it is our constant addiction to hope—even our pontifications that hope is our moral obligation, that have allowed us to kick the climate can down the road until it exploded in our faces. We can thank both the chimera of certainty and our addiction to hope for delivering us to our current ecocidal destination.

Addicts who have spent many years in recovery often report that while they had some indication of what sober living could bring them, they have joyously discovered dimensions of their own being that they could not have known in a state of addiction. Full disclosure: I'm here to take away your hope in exchange for your discovery of the creativity, compassion, connection, and courage that are available when you give up hope.

Author, farmer, and cultural activist Stephen Jenkinson offers a unique and exhilarating redefinition of the word *catastrophe*. In his superb, wordsmithing fashion, he analyzes the ancient origins of the word which are remarkably relevant to this moment in the history of our planet. Noting the prefix, *kata*, and noting the fact that it is a preposition carrying the "volatility, the direction, the thrust and purpose of that part of speech, it answers the question 'Where?'" The answer is "down" or "below." In ancient Greek mysteries, "down" or "below" did not mean "hell." Rather, it meant, "beneath what we're ordinarily granted to see." It pointed to a descent—a descent with a purpose. It also carried the connotation that the descent was not merely "down" but also "in." Greek mysteries were all about descending into the depths of the soul in order to experience the sacred, the profound, the divine.[4]

Then comes the suffix *strophe*, whose older meaning was "a thing braided together or woven or gathered in a pattern and strategy." When joined with *kata*, we can infer that the descent that takes us downward and inward is one that has meaning and purpose; it is not done in isolation. It is a descent into the deepest Mysteries of the universe. It involves many parts of the individual psyche, as well as reciprocity and kinship with external allies. Or as Jenkinson summarizes:

> *Catastrophe* means that, yes, your descent into the Mysteries will be a solitary one, and yes, you will have companions nonetheless.[5]

Our current climate *cata-strophe* is compelling us into a descent we cannot control that will plunge us into the depths of the mystical experiences of our own sacred being. Moreover, we are not the first humans to have experienced *cata-strophe*, nor do we need to experience it alone. We can and must descend together with companions.

Our death-grasp on "hope" invariably precludes the possibility of a meaningful descent into the Mysteries into which we are being drawn in these dangerous times. It also prevents our being "braided together" or "woven" in community as we descend.

These are extraordinarily confusing times, but as Meg Wheatley asserts, "We can't be creative if we refuse to be confused. Change always starts with confusion; cherished interpretations must dissolve to make way for the new. Of course it's scary to give up what we know, but the abyss is where newness lives."[6]

Yes, the abyss *is* where newness lives, but compassion, connection, and courage also live there. The more we attend to these, the less focused on certainty and hope we will need to be. *In fact, hope is not something you do; it's something you choose to be.*

Both the "we're fucked" crowd and the techno-optimists who believe they will save us argue with friends or colleagues about hope or hopelessness in the face of climate catastrophe. But as Wheatley writes, "It's people, our relationships, that give meaning to our struggles. If we free ourselves from hope and fear, it isn't outcomes that matter. It's our relationships that give meaning to our struggles. If we free ourselves from hope and fear, from having to succeed, we discover that it becomes easier to love. We stop scapegoating, we stop blaming, and we stop being disappointed in each other. We realize that we truly are in this together, and that's all that matters."[7]

Can we do the work that calls us without demanding that it produce results? Can we do it knowing that it may not produce results in our lifetime, but may at a later time?

When we embrace both uncertainty and hopelessness, we give up needing to have solid ground to stand on in a world where there really *is* no solid ground—and if there is, it's already turning to mush.

Abandoning certainty and hope liberates us to discover roles for ourselves that make a difference in alleviating suffering and lovingly stewarding the Earth, even as humanity appears to be careening toward the brick wall of extinction.

What Meg Wheatley is ultimately offering is a perspective that resembles Jung's notion of holding the tension of opposites. We consent to live with uncertainty and hopelessness, alongside with meaning-making, purpose, joy, beauty, and compassion, while at the same time noticing that ecocide and extinction are breathing down our necks. This has never been a task for the faint of heart.

Therefore, we must persevere in asking the two questions that will not relent: *Who do I want to be? What did I come here to do?* In the end, they have little or nothing to do with hope or certainty as we have known them in the past.

FIERCE PRACTICES

These practices are more effective when we make time to journal and quietly reflect on them without interruption.

- How do you feel when you hear Meg Wheatley's words about hope?
- How do you imagine it would feel to give up hope for the future of our planet?
- If you have already abandoned hope, what was that like for you in the past, and what is it like today?
- What roles have you discovered for yourself that help you alleviate suffering and care for people and the planet?
- Who do you want to be?
- What did you come here to do?

CHAPTER 10

COMPASSION IS NOT
FOR SISSIES

When we practice generating compassion, we can expect to experience our fear of pain. Compassion practice is daring. It involves learning to relax and allow ourselves to move gently toward what scares us. The trick to doing this is to stay with emotional distress without tightening into aversion, to let fear soften us rather than harden into resistance. —Pema Chodron[1]

Everyone carries a shadow, and the less it is embodied in the individual's conscious life, the blacker and denser it is. At all counts, it forms an unconscious snag, thwarting our most well-meant intentions. —Carl Jung[2]

In 2015, when I decided to sit in the streets of Boulder, Colorado and beg alongside my homeless friend so that I could give the money to him, but more importantly, experience the humiliation of begging and appearing to be homeless as well, I didn't understand that after that experience, I would never be the same. While begging in the street felt absolutely demeaning, I soon discovered how daring it actually was. Externally, I could have been arrested for panhandling alongside my friend, and that was scary. But it wasn't as terrifying as it was for my ego to engage in what it had previously considered scandalous, denigrating behavior.

Contrary to popular opinion, compassionate people are not "bleeding hearts" or "lily-livered liberals." Practicing compassion requires courage on many levels because it invariably incites pushback from oneself, from the external world, and even from those to whom one expresses compassion. However, practicing compassion is not a popularity contest. We practice compassion because it is the right thing to do, because we cannot *not* practice it, and because in the end, we taste the sweet nectar of interconnectedness and claim our place within Indra's Net.

Most of us believe that in the throes of a collapsing society, if we survive or as we are endeavoring to survive, we will assist other people who need help and welcome their assisting us. We believe that if we survive a harrowing disaster such as a tornado, wildfire, flood, or earthquake, we will practice compassion toward our fellow humans. While our fellow humans, for the most part, will be grateful for our assistance, many won't be. Many will continue to deny climate chaos or even blame those who have been warning others about it. Certainly, compassion is not likely to be the only emotion we experience during the traumatizing experiences related to climate disaster. We will need to also cope with our own fear, anger, and grief. Amid the disruptions, we will be compelled to confront our own resentments toward those who refused to take climate chaos seriously and who will continue to do so in the face of horrific devastation.

In those circumstances, we will be mightily tempted to dispense incessant "I told you so's" or inwardly gloat over the misfortunes of others who have been steeped in denial. Therefore, we need to ask ourselves: If we are not practicing compassion now, why do we believe that we will practice it then?

In my work I often sit with people who spew rage at the human race for the suffering it has visited on the Earth. Their contempt for their fellow humans appears unbounded. Some want nothing to do with humans and invest their compassion only in animals. I understand this. I know how seductive it is to withhold compassion from other humans.

Compassion is possible only if we viscerally experience the fact that we are all in the soup of climate chaos together. It is *not* possible if we are setting ourselves apart from or above the rest of our species. I submit that the more we do so, the less likely we are to have compassion for ourselves, and without compassion for ourselves, it is impossible to practice compassion with anyone else. As Pema Chodron writes, "Compassion becomes real when we recognize our shared humanity."[3]

African American Christian theologian Dr. Jacqui Lewis writes that:

> In any relationship, fierce love causes us to cross boundaries and borders to discover one another, to support one another, to heal one another. When we do this, when we go crazy with affection, and offer wild kindness to our neighbor across the street or across the globe, we make a new kind of space between us. We make space for discovery and curiosity, for learning and growing. We make space for sharing stories and being changed by what we share. This is the space of the *border*, of *mestizaje* [mixed race], of both/and. . . . We can learn to see the world not only through our own stories, through our own eyes, but also through the stories and worldview of the so-called other. . . . We simply must open our eyes, look across the room, the street, the division, the border—and reach out to that

neighbor, offering our hand, our compassion, and our heart.[4]

CONFRONTING THE HUMAN SHADOW

In my book *Dark Gold: The Human Shadow and the Global Crisis*, I wrote extensively about the human shadow and how it manifests both personally and culturally. More recently, Jungian psychologist Connie Zweig wrote in *The Inner Work of Age* that:

The shadow is our personal unconscious, that part of our mind that is behind or beneath our conscious awareness. We can't gaze at it directly. It's like a blind spot in our field of vision. Because it is hidden, we need to learn how to seek it. To do so, we need to be able to see in the dark...When we are children, the conscious ego and the unconscious shadow develop in tandem. Each is reinforced by the messages, even the glances, of parents, teachers, clergy, siblings, and friends when we try to gain love and approval. If our sadness is shamed, it is exiled into the shadow. If our anger is punished, it is pushed into the shadow. Our ego develops to accommodate the loss of those authentic feelings. The shadow is like a darkroom in which our feelings, dreams, and images lie dormant. Shadow-work is like the process of development in which our feelings, dreams, and images come back to life.

When we learn how to establish a conscious relationship with those parts of ourselves that are outside of awareness, we can attune to our many inner voices and detect which can be guides for us now—and which can sabotage our dreams. We can learn to slow down, turn within with curiosity, and open to what's calling to us without dismissing it—and without being taken over by it. That's what I call "romancing" the shadow.[5]

Anyone who desires to deepen their compassion but is unwilling to do shadow work will be thwarted or distorted at every turn by this unconscious aspect of ourselves that can sabotage our commitment to compassion and possibly cause us to express its very opposite. Sadly, this attitude toward shadow work is often articulated by people or groups claiming to follow a spiritual path. They prefer not to "sully themselves" with the shadow, "avoid dark thoughts," and "live in the light." As a result, they spiritually and emotionally bypass not only one of the fundamental aspects of the human psyche, but by avoiding shadow work, they abandon a golden opportunity for consciousness transformation and the deepening of their compassion.

THE WÉTIKO PANDEMIC

Many people familiar with my work are also familiar with Paul Levy's work on *wétiko* as articulated in his first book on the topic, *Dispelling Wétiko* and his more recent work, *Wétiko: Healing the Mind-Virus that Plagues Our World*. Levy defines *wétiko* as a "cannibalizing force driven by insatiable greed, appetite without satisfaction, consumption as an end in itself, and war for its own sake against other tribes, species, and nature, and even against an individual's own humanity."[6]

While *wétiko* can destroy our species, it is at the same time a potential catalyst for our evolution as a species. We don't dispel it by fighting it externally. As Levy says, "The fact that *wétiko* is the expression of something inside us means that the cure for *wétiko* is likewise within us."[7]

When we rail against other humans for their willful ignorance, stupidity, or participation in destroying the planet, our perception is only partially accurate. Even if they have devoted their entire lives to fossil fuel extraction or mountain top removal or polluting rivers and oceans, their behavior is just a symptom of their shadow—and our own. While we may not like them and absolutely do not need to, we do need to notice that we too could have made similar choices and probably would have had we lived their life experiences. Moreover, none of us is exempt from having participated in ecocide directly or indirectly through our own poor choices throughout our lives.

I have noticed that among those who follow my work on the shadow, and who also follow Levy's work on *wétiko*, many resist doing inner shadow work and prefer to continue pointing the finger at the rest of humanity for murdering the planet. However, the more we find ourselves enraged with the human species, the more we need to turn inward and notice our own Inner Polluter, Inner Pillager, or Inner Robber Baron. Even if we are not expressing these "characters" externally, they are part of the shadow. We can begin healing their presence in our psyches by simply being curious about them. We can then deepen our exploration by developing a relationship with them. (Practices for this are offered at the end of this chapter.)

What is more, the wisdom traditions of Buddhism, mystical Christianity, and the depth psychology of Carl Jung, as well as myriad indigenous traditions, point to and can assist us in deepening our understanding of *wétiko*. Any spiritual teaching that encourages us to "stay positive" and "avoid darkness" is enabling *wétiko* to further infect our consciousness. "Because *wétiko* is a psychic blindness," says Levy, "the cure for *wétiko* starts with seeing it—both seeing how it operates in the world and also tracking how it covertly operates within our own being."[8]

Wétiko operates both internally in the individual and collectively in nations and communities. In fact, every individual and every group of individuals has its shadow and can be manipulated by it if it is not explored and worked with. When we refuse to do the inner work of shadow healing, we invariably project the shadow onto another individual or group. In fact, this is essentially how the world runs—masses of individuals refusing to heal the shadow and projecting it onto other persons, cultures, and nations. Not only does such scapegoating invariably lead to war, but it is also inherently dehumanizing.

Hannah Arendt, from whom we will be hearing more later in this book, noted that every form of totalitarianism is rooted in dehumanization.[9] She emphasizes that authoritarian individuals and governments project their shadow onto those they consider to be like animals, vermin, parasites, microbes, germs, and cancers. In other words, they are seen as living poison that needs to be destroyed. Levy emphasizes that:

> The process of individuation and the development of consciousness necessarily requires the withdrawal of as many of our projections as we can possibly muster. That necessarily means to withdraw our shadow projections, which involves recognizing and accepting 'the other' in ourselves. Once we recognize and withdraw our projections, we can no longer blame other people for our problems.[10]

When we own our shadow, commit to healing it, no matter how unpleasant that experience may be, we discover that humanity is us, and we are humanity—that nature is us, and we are nature. Shadow healing work, above any other work available to us, profoundly and unalterably connects us intimately with ourselves, with other humans, and with the Earth.

It is only through shadow work that we successfully stop projecting and "otherizing" and genuinely begin experiencing ourselves as being in the soup with all of humanity. Is this not our deepest need as we stand on the threshold of potential extinction? The result, Levy assures us, is an inestimably deepened compassion for ourselves—all of ourselves, including the parts we are ashamed of—as well as compassion for all living beings. This, above all else, is what it means to become whole.

By holding the tension of opposites within ourselves—by recognizing the beautiful and benevolent parts of ourselves alongside the dark and despicable parts— we become more skillful in holding the tension of opposites externally in a world where the very best in humanity and the very worst in us is incessantly on display, and where we are incapable of predicting our fate with certainty.

FIERCE PRACTICES

These practices are more effective when we make time to journal and quietly reflect on them without interruption.

- Where are you practicing compassion in your life?
- How are you practicing compassion with yourself?
- What do you already know about your shadow?
- What upsets you about other humans?
- Notice your anger at people in climate denial, people who are blatantly polluting and pillaging. Is there a part of you that quietly gloats when extreme weather disasters strike because it makes you "right" regarding what you believe about climate chaos?
- Take time to sit quietly with your anger toward these people. Notice where you feel it in your body.

Are you aware of a part of yourself that is like them?
Write down everything you know about that part.

- A SUPER-FIERCE PRACTICE: As you sit with the
  part of yourself (see above) that you have
  connected to people you are angry with for causing
  climate chaos and collapse, ask it to speak to you
  and listen to it. What do you learn from it? What
  would you like to say to it? Write about your
  experience with this practice.

CHAPTER II

TRANSFORMING THE CONCEPT OF "CARE" AND "COMMUNITY"

Kindness is made possible by accepting paradox. Let our entire existence be a protest against servitude to a worldview devoid of mercy on the one hand and unquestioning addiction to the delusion of certainty on the other hand. Embrace paradox! Be happy! Embrace the humility of not knowing! Do not believe in any promise based on anything less than the experience of unconditional love. In other words, adopt the canine spiritual philosophy of life! —Frank Schaeffer, author of *Fall in Love, Have Children, Stay Put, Save the Planet, Be Happy*[1]

My religion is kindness. —His Holiness, Dalai Lama[2]

This past year, my friend and colleague Frank Schaeffer wrote the book *Fall In Love, Have Children, Stay Put, Save the Planet, Be Happy*. At first blush, such a title may sound narcissistic, privileged, and totally oblivious to our predicament. However, Schaeffer offers a new definition of caring based in evolution, not morality. His book is a manifesto *against* sacrificing love in order to advance one's career, income, and status and *for* "the evolutionary fact of the need for relationships, family, and connection—things that are of intrinsic value to humans."[3] In other words, "evolution's rule for success is this: cooperate, be friendly, help others, and survive."

Before you conclude that Schaeffer is clueless about our trajectory toward extinction, I want to affirm that his perspective is exactly the one we are going to need in a collapsing world. In that world, we will rapidly discover that *care*, not status quo, is what makes the world go round.

Schaeffer sheltered in place during the Covid pandemic with his wife and grandchildren and spent many months engaging in childcare, cooking, helping with homework, and caring for the home. Most importantly, he allowed himself to be schooled by these experiences rather than resisting them. Thus, in his 2021 book he shares many aspects of the deep transformation that the dramatic shift from being a "career man" to becoming a "care man" evoked in him.

Which brings us to the question: What would it be like to live in a society organized around *care* instead of acquisition? While that may seem unrealistic or even unimaginable at the moment, consider a world in which climate upheaval and extreme weather are producing disasters monthly, weekly, or even daily. Imagine a world or community in which people cannot merely relocate because no venue is exempt from climate chaos, and people are forced to shelter in place? Consider the likelihood that communities regularly pelted with extreme weather events eventually despair of even attempting to rebuild and will make do with what little shelter or livelihood they have. While basic survival will become their fundamental *modus operandi*, people will *not* survive unless they care for each other.

Schaeffer asks:

What if we changed our definition of success so none of us faced social pressures or economic pressures during our children's little child years (say birth to four years old and preschool) to conform to a pro-business, one-size-fits-all, Goldman Sachs'–style model of life focused on our job title? What if families stuck together so grandparents were there to help? What if we didn't see ourselves defined by "a robust and fulfilling full-time career" first but rather by the robust and fulfilling quality of our most important relationships and the FUN they spin off as surely as fire generates heat? What if parents also received a baseline of financial Social Security–type support while their children were ages birth to four, so they...could afford to stay home and have the pleasure of caring for their kids? What if our society transformed into one that does not revolve around purchasing; one in which our primary role is not as consumers armed with our commonly deployed credit cards?[4]

I suspect that in an unraveling world where climate chaos and the collapse of systems prevail, this scenario will become not a question but a lifestyle. I doubt that in such a world, parents would receive any type of financial support. What is more likely is that community members, out of necessity, would need to support one another in terms of accessing the basic necessities of life and providing childcare, eldercare, healthcare, education, and emotional support.

Schaeffer argues that "if the Coronavirus taught us anything, it's what our actual needs are. College is nice, jobs are necessary—but we need connection. We need community. We need to be nurtured and supported."[5] We also need to stay put. For decades, corporations have been shuffling employees all over the planet, while numerous ecologists and environmental authors, such as Sharon Blackie, are now telling us to fall in love with a place and "rise rooted" by serving and caring for it.

Perhaps you find yourself resisting words in the title of Schaeffer's book—like "have children" and "be happy." I am often asked how I feel about people having children in a world on the brink of extinction. I do not have children of my own, so if I speak against the notion, I will probably be discounted, and if I speak in favor of it, I may be accused of being heartlessly in denial of climate chaos and its dire implications for future generations. After reading Roy Scranton's *Learning to Die in the Anthropocene*, I would never have imagined that he would choose to have children, but he did. Of this, he says:

> I'm committed to life in this world, the world I live in, in all its stupidity and suffering, because this world is the one everyone else lives in too: my colleagues and students, my friends and family, my partner and daughter. This world is the only one in which my choices have meaning. And this world, doomed as it is, is the only one that offers joy.[6]

Scranton argues that what matters is not whether or not we have children but whether we commit to live ethically in a broken world—"giving up any claims to innocence or moral purity." I doubt that Scranton had shadow work in mind when he wrote those words, but I do. Isn't it our claims to innocence and moral purity that cause us to judge those who have children during our predicament?

Even more wisely, and echoing Schaffer, Scranton writes:

> I can't protect my daughter from the future and I can't even promise her a better life. All I can do is teach her: teach her how to care, how to be kind and how to live within the limits of nature's grace. I can teach her to be tough but resilient,

adaptable, and prudent, because she's going to have to struggle for what she needs. But I also need to teach her to fight for what's right, because none of us is in this alone. I need to teach her that all things die, even her and me and her mother and the world we know, but that coming to terms with this difficult truth is the beginning of wisdom.[7]

As we prepare ourselves emotionally and spiritually for an increasingly broken world, we must teach ourselves and others "how to care, how to be kind, and how to live within the limits of nature's grace." I believe that shadow work and practicing compassion are extraordinary curricula for creating a culture based on care and deep community.

We need to familiarize ourselves with care systems in other parts of the world so that when no systems in our location are available, we have some idea of how to put them in place. For example, in the United States in 2021, we are witnessing implacable resistance to human infrastructure efforts in Congress such as the Build Back Better Act to provide child tax credits to parents, expanded funds for daycare, and other enhancements of care systems in America. Amid the delusional religion of uber-individualism which deplores public health in the midst of the worst pandemic we have witnessed in more than one hundred years, the notion of the common good is now on life-support.

Ask the victims of climate disasters how important the common good is to them. Very few will say that it doesn't matter to them because without caring for each other, they cannot and will not survive. Mutual caring and support in a location pummeled by disaster is instinctive because it is evolutionary—human survival and well-being depend on it.

Tragically, it appears that deadly disasters are required for many Americans to care for anyone who does not live under the same roof. However, before climate catastrophe compels us to care for those we don't even know, let us begin and continue caring for the suffering "strangers" we encounter, who nevertheless, inhabit our world. The Hindu sage Ramana Maharishi, when asked how we should treat others, replied, "There *are* no others."

FIERCE PRACTICES

These practices are more effective when we make time to journal and quietly reflect on them without interruption.

- From your perspective, what would a society organized around care look like? Take plenty of time to reflect on this.
- In a collapsed or collapsing society, what kinds of care can you offer? What kinds of care can you offer now?
- How might you need to be cared for in a severely disrupted world?
- What have been your experiences of caring and being cared for during the pandemic?

CHAPTER 12

I LOVE YOU, SON, BUT I LOVE FOSSIL FUELS MORE

Young people must hold older generations accountable. —Greta Thunberg[1]

One night while making dinner, my 21-year-old son brought up how hopeless he was feeling about some climate news he'd read and what it meant for his future. I just stopped what I was doing because I could see he was emotionally distraught. So that was about me being as attentive as you would be with a 2-year-old, but with someone 20 years older, saying, 'Tell me more.' And I just listened to his despair. —Mary DeMocker, author of *The Parents' Guide to Climate Revolution: 100 Ways to Build a Fossil-Free Future, Raise Empowered Kids, and Still Get a Good Night's Sleep*[2]

Recently, while perusing Facebook, I noticed a cartoon showing a very tall man looking down at a very small little boy with a caption that read, "I love you, son, but I love fossil fuels more." Although the naked honesty of the cartoon was disturbing, it captured the truth that no parent or grandparent wants to own. I say this not to shame anyone but to remind members of older generations that we are accountable to our descendants. While some may bristle and declare their innocence, climate chaos and climate catastrophe are the expert witnesses that shatter our imagined guilelessness.

I used to receive questions regularly from parents concerned with how to talk to their kids about climate chaos. Today, I receive many more questions from parents asking me how to respond to kids who bring the subject up first. I also receive many more questions about whether to have children at all. Few authors could be accused of a more doomer-ish perspective than Roy Scranton, the author of *How to Die in the Anthropocene*, whose perspective on having children was noted above and is not one that readers of his book might expect.

Even if you choose not to have children, you will likely encounter a young person or young people who are angry at older generations for allowing climate chaos to happen.

The worldwide Extinction Rebellion movement is not a youth movement *per se*. But it includes a youth wing which proclaims: "We are rebelling against the government for climate and ecological justice. We cannot trust the government to protect our futures and our homes. We are for immediate systematic change that prioritizes the life of our planet and the people on it. As the youth, we are taking our future into our own hands."[3]

If you have children, teach them early on to appreciate and protect nature. Even small children can become accustomed to being in nature, learning from and about nature, and defending it. Teaching children to explore the environment is likely to decrease time spent in front of screens, increase their engagement with the natural world, and motivate them to advocate for it. We should not expect all youth to be Greta

Thunbergs, but we can inspire them to appreciate and advocate for the planet they inhabit.

Emma Patee, writer for *Wired Magazine*, offers wise advice for parents when discussing climate change with older children, including sample phrases that might be helpful, such as:

- *"I know this is big and overwhelming, but I also really believe there's so much we can do to rise to the challenge and make a difference."*
- *"I don't have all the answers, and I'm learning about this the same as you are, but I know it's important that we keep talking, and I'm really open to whatever you're feeling or thinking."*
- *"What would feel supportive? Do you want help learning more, or help getting involved, or just having me be a person you can share your feelings with and know I won't judge you or try to fix it?"*

As a parent, it's easy to feel like you have to have all the answers or be able to make your child feel better when they're upset. That's why talking about the climate crisis can be especially difficult for parents. It can be tempting to change the subject or avoid talking about it altogether. But keep this in mind: Your kid doesn't need you to have answers or solve their feelings. They just need you to show up, ask questions, and listen to the answers.[4]

Children may challenge the ways we are responding to climate chaos. They may point to our hypocrisy, our environmental transgressions, or our lingering indicators of denial. Conversely, a young person may indicate no interest in the topic or not be as proactive as we would like them to be. Regardless of how our children respond or do not respond to climate chaos, they offer us teaching moments on a continuum, from comments or questions that may hurt to those that may feel utterly delightful. However much we may disagree, we as adults are accountable to them and must remain emotionally available to support them as they struggle with the perilous future we have left them.

FIERCE PRACTICES

These practices are more effective when we make time to journal and quietly reflect on them without interruption.

- Whether or not you have children, as an adult, you have a responsibility to younger generations to model Earth stewardship. Who are the younger people in your life with whom you can discuss climate chaos and support them in actively responding to it?
- Ask a younger person how they feel about climate chaos and make an effort to simply listen to them. Notice how you feel as they speak.
- If your child is involved in any kind of environmental activism, let them know that you are available to support them, and ask them if they would like your help, even if you believe that their efforts are miniscule and will make no difference at all. If they welcome your help, get involved. Likewise, if you are involved with environmental activism, ask your child if they would like to be involved with you.

CHAPTER 13
COMING OF AGE AT THE END OF AN AGE

Perhaps, as Carl Jung suggested, if we hold the tension of opposites and let them simmer for a while, rather than choosing one side and banishing the other into denial, a novel third possibility will emerge: the capacity to become a true Elder, who does not think in black-and-white terms, splitting good and bad, projecting one or the other, but who holds the tension of shadow and light—who is both nourished and nourishing. —Connie Zweig[1]

What should I be doing with whatever is left to me? If I'm capable of anything, how should I lean upon it now? That is not idle contemplation these days, if it ever was. That IS my days. — Stephen Jenkinson, *Coming of Age: The Case for Elderhood in a Time of Trouble*[2]

Catastrophe is the job description of an elder. Be a catastrophe for this age. —Stephen Jenkinson[3]

On the one hand, aging has never been easier in industrial societies. Never before have we had the quantity or quality of assisted living and long-term care facilities available to the senior demographic. Before the global pandemic, travel was never more manageable. These days, however, if grandparents cannot travel to visit grandchildren, Zoom is the magic word. A plethora of seniors living longer lives has engendered the explosion of retirement and senior care industries that deliver more convenience, comfort, and companionship than aging individuals could have imagined a century ago.

On its face, we are promised that aging can be not only hassle-free but also fun. Yet in the inner world, another story is likely unfolding. It is fascinating to notice how elderhood is perceived in this culture. In fact, the word "elderhood" is rarely used. We are "senior citizens," "living into our 'golden' years," or sometimes, the less formal and more specific term for us is used: *boomers*.

The culture expects certain things of us and projects many *more* things *onto* us. This is a time of retirement, when it is assumed we will develop or deepen our hobbies, revel in our leisure, travel extensively, or perhaps create new projects to fill in the time we used to devote to working. However, nothing is expected of us more than spending time with our grand-children.

But what if we don't have grandchildren? What if we lack the resources to travel? What if our mission in life is getting ourselves to medical appointments and to the bathroom?

If we can't do the things expected of us in our aging years, who are we? Is there something more to us than what we can or can't do?

In indigenous cultures, people of a certain age group are

seen as elders. "Elder," in those cultures, means something very different from merely "older." In fact, for the indigenous man or woman, elder is a special role that one consciously claims and steps into with great intention. Tribal culture prepares its members for the role throughout their lives by supporting the gathering and distilling of soul wisdom. It is important to understand that anyone can be "older," but becoming an elder in the community is a title reserved for the woman or man who has cultivated wisdom and imparted it, not just to younger people, but to the community at large. What is also true is that because elder is not the same as older, people who are not "senior citizens" and who have cultivated deep wisdom may live and move as elders in the community even before they reach a certain age. Just as we know people who have lived many years but don't seem very wise, we probably know younger people who seem wise beyond their years.

CHOOSING ELDERHOOD

Obviously, the indigenous perspective of elderhood is dramatically different from the story our culture tells us about aging. The indigenous elder may travel, have hobbies, create projects, and spend time with grandchildren, but they identify as a *carrier of wisdom* that benefits not only themselves, but all living beings. What does that mean?

Being a wise elder is more than the capacity to score cheap airline tickets to Europe. In fact, quite naturally, the authentic elder metabolizes their life experience—his or her own pain and suffering, the sorrow and wounding of the Earth, the unhealed trauma in the community, his or her unique mountain of regrets about the past, and above all, the soul-wrenching grief of their entire lifetime. The elder knows in their bones that grief is love—that we grieve because love has been there all along, regardless of how broken, estranged, or defeated we may feel.

The wise elder may spend time with his or her grandchildren if they have grandchildren, but not for the sake of just "spending time." The elder will not preach, but they are available for teaching moments that parents may overlook or be too busy to utilize, and in those moments, the elder is, above all, simply present with the situation. In fact, the *presence* of the elder is what matters most, whether or not words are needed. It is what will be remembered by those for whom it made a difference. The elder holds treasure that "youngers" may not yet be able to access.

The wise elder understands that because of humanity's abuse of the Earth, we are living at the end of an age—the age of raping, pillaging, and exhausting the planet. As the climate becomes more chaotic, human systems will invariably collapse. The pandemic has proven this already, and it continues to reveal that we will be forced to change our living arrangements. Defining ourselves by our work, our material possessions, our ability to travel, our degrees, and our finances is over. *What the world now desperately needs is not more aging tourists, but more women and men who are committed to becoming wise elders who are purposefully living the gifts they brought with them to this Earth.*

Not unlike parenting, being an elder in any capacity is often a thankless endeavor. Resistance to the aging process itself often results in people projecting their shadow on the elder. Like a loving parent, the elder is challenged to hold the world and her community in her heart despite pushback.

ELDERHOOD AT ANY AGE

Younger readers need not feel discouraged that they have lived fewer years. Since elderhood is not about age but about depth of wisdom, we must not fail to notice that many younger individuals have come into the world with stunning wisdom which has erupted in youth and is now available to people of all ages. The Extinction Rebellion movement is populated with masses of youth who, like Greta Thunberg, are passionately committed to healing the Earth and preventing the extinction of species. The gifts of aging can be incipient in youth and may develop more fully as the body and mind mature. However, regardless of where the hands on the biological clock rest, the world needs individuals who are willing to claim their elderhood at any age.

In the aging process we are limited by weaker bodies and declining energy, but we do not have to limit our final years to living out the story of aging that this culture has given us. Whether we are able-bodied, disabled, or living in long-term care, we have *inner* work to do in our elderhood. In fact, inner work is a significant facet of what defines an elder. His or her task is the ongoing development, distillation, and delivery of wisdom—not information, but wisdom acquired from living —finding and making meaning in one's life experience and sharing one's gifts with the community, even in the face of myriad limitations.

The culture's story of aging is that we are always "young at heart" and can continue growing and improving and thriving indefinitely. Every aspect of industrial society's aging is set up to be a kind of geriatric personal growth retreat where people write and mouth affirmations about "not getting older but getting better." Our personal shadow and the cultural shadow that the senior living industry assiduously works to conceal is that we are approaching our death in a culture that does not understand the role of the elder because it is frantically obsessed with staying young and invincible. When the naked truth is told, in this culture, we have no value, and we are old, wrinkled, smelly, and frail—all of which is an abhorrent reminder that life is fragile, and that all of us are moving steadily toward death.

However, Stephen Jenkinson, a skillful truth-teller and remarkable sage of our times, asserts:

> Elder is not the one who grows without end, come what may, but the one who causes depth and fullness by being deep and full, the one who prompts and is prompted by ebbing, by the failure and the end of growth. Considered in this way, a life lived chafing at limits is a life that thwarts the advent of *old*, and of its crowning achievement, *elder*.[4]

In other words, says Jenkinson, we are "deepened by diminishment."

If we allow it, we consciously step into elderhood when the human ego is curtailed—tapered and tempered by sacred encounters with the deeper Self to which we open, perhaps for the first time. That opening may release the floodgates of grief, regret, remorse, and above all, reverence for our lives and our potential, enabling us to be the light within the dark places we inhabit and to do what our heart calls us to do within the physical limitations we cannot transcend.

FIERCE PRACTICES

These practices are more effective when we make time to journal and quietly reflect on them without interruption.

- Summarize your inner work of aging. What additional work do you want/need to do?
- Whether you are young or old, what does "stepping into elderhood" look like for you?
- What is one aspect of your acquired wisdom that you are offering the world?
- What limitations of aging are you facing?
- What are those limitations teaching you?
- What gifts of wisdom are you sharing with the community?

CHAPTER 14

EARTH CARE, SELF-CARE: SACRED NATURE

All life, mind, and sense
Come from the One.
All space, light, air, fire and water
Come from the One.
Indeed, from the One comes all.
—Mundaka Upanishad[1]

I used to think the top environmental problems were biodiversity loss, ecosystems collapse and climate change. I thought that with 30 years of good science we could address those problems. But I was wrong. The top environmental problems are selfishness, greed and apathy... and to deal with those we need a spiritual and cultural transformation and we, (Lawyers) and scientists, don´t know how to do that. —Gus Speth, American environmental lawyer and advocate who co-founded the Natural Resources Defense Council[2]

This alienation from the spirituality of the Earth goes so deep that it is beyond our conscious mode of awareness...The universe is the supreme manifestation of the sacred. —Thomas Berry[3]

Mystical experience in nature—those moments when you sense your interconnection with all things—are more than just interesting encounters. They are invitations into relationship. Beyond caring for creation or stewarding Earth's "resources," it is entering into an actual relationship with particular places and beings of the living world that can provide an embodied, rooted foundation for transformation. The global shift necessary to actually survive the crises we've created depends on a deep inner change. —Victoria Loorz, *Church of the Wild: How Nature Invites Us into the Sacred*[4]

When I published my book *Sacred Demise: Walking the Spiritual Path of Industrial Civilization's Collapse* in 2009, some people were taken aback by my use of the word "sacred" in the title. They assumed that "sacred" and "religious" were synonymous for me and that somehow I should be viewed with suspicion. When I facilitated workshops and author events, I took great care to explain that for me, "sacred" had nothing to do with "religious," and I often clarified the difference by pointing to the use of "sacred" in indigenous traditions.

Today, one of my favorite authors is John Philip Newell, a Celtic teacher and Christian minister whose book *Sacred Earth, Sacred Soul* is like cool water poured onto the dry, parched, rationalistic desert of our postmodern, dualistic consciousness. Dear to Newell's heart is his immersion in the West's truly indigenous tradition, Celtic culture and spirituality. Of this he writes:

Sacred is the right word to convey this Celtic way of seeing, because it is a word that is not bound by religion. Inside the walls of religious practice, we speak of sacred scripture or sacred music, for instance, but way beyond those walls we also speak of the sacred universe or sacred moments. The word points with reverence to the divine essence of life and the true nature of relationship. When we speak of something as sacred, we are offering it ultimate respect. We are honoring it. We also invoke something of the power and authority of this word when we use the related term sacrilege to speak of the wrongs that are being done to the earth, to the creatures, and to other human beings. Etymologically, sacrilege means to try to take possession of the sacred, to use it for one's own ends rather than to reverence it.[5]

With a truly indigenous sensibility, Newell argues:

In Celtic wisdom, the sacred is as present on earth as it is in heaven, as immanent as it is transcendent, as human as it is divine, as physical as it is spiritual. The sacred can be breathed in, tasted, touched, heard, and seen as much in the body of the earth and the body of another living being as in the body of religion. It is the true essence of all life.[6]

In other words, from the perspective of Oneness, the spiritual cannot be separated from the physical, mental, or emotional aspects of our humanity.

EMPIRE VS. EARTH

Typical of the clash of all empires with indigenous traditions, the Roman Empire could not abide with the Celtic worldview for many reasons, not the least of which was Celtic reverence for the Earth as sacred. Newell writes that:

> All of these themes of sacredness clashed with the ways empire worked. They were like seeds of radicalism. The sacredness of the human soul: people are not just there to be controlled and used, but should be reverenced and related to. The sacredness of nature: we cannot do whatever we wish to the body of the earth, but are to honor it as our own body. The sacredness of spiritual practice: truth is not just dispensed from above by those who are in power, but accessed from deep within by everyone. The sacredness of wisdom: one nation, or culture, or religion does not have a monopoly on wisdom; it is to be found in all people, all cultures, all religions. The sacredness of compassion: we are to see and feel and act for others as we see and feel and act for ourselves. All of this challenged the inequities upon which the empire was built.[7]

Humans are unequivocally at the point of environmental catastrophe and potential extinction of life on this planet because we have dichotomized the Sacred and the Earth. We tend to think of this dichotomy arising with the dawn of the Scientific Revolution of the seventeenth and eighteenth centuries. However, the estrangement began with the slow industrialization of agricultural societies and the rise of empires that increasingly realized how useful religions and spiritual traditions could be in their quest for land and power. With time, the reverence for a "sacred Earth" was supplanted by the notion of "private property" and "real estate." As the visceral connection with Earth diminished, so too did intimacy with the human soul.

Thomas Berry, who stopped calling himself a *theologian*

and began calling himself a *geologian,* notes that this process
has culminated in our current global predicament.

> If we think...that the changes taking place in our time are
> simply another moment in the series of transformations that
> passes from classical-Mediterranean times through the
> medieval era to the industrial and modern periods, then we
> are missing the real magnitude of the changes taking place.
> We are, in fact, at the end of a religious-civilizational period.
> By virtue of our new knowledge, we are changing our most
> basic relations to the world about us. We are changing the
> chemistry of the planet. These changes are of a unique order
> of magnitude.
>
> Our new acquaintance with the universe as an irre-
> versible developmental process can be considered the most
> significant religious, spiritual, and scientific event since the
> emergence of the more complex civilizations some five thou-
> sand years ago. At the same time, we are bringing about the
> devastation of Earth such as the planet has never experi-
> enced in the four and a half billion years of its formation.[8]

Berry would argue, as would Newell, that our spirituality is
Earth-derived. "The human and the Earth," Berry insists, "are
totally implicated, each in the other. If there is no spirituality
in the Earth, then there is no spirituality in ourselves."

In recent years I have come to believe that any so-called
"spiritual path" that does not emerge out of and revel in our
inextricable connection with Earth does not merit the term
"spiritual path." Berry articulates this brilliantly:

Ultimately, spirituality is a mode of being in which not
only the divine and the human commune with each other but
through which we discover ourselves in the universe, and the
universe discovers itself in us.[9]

IT'S ALL ABOUT EARTH

With few exceptions, modern, Western religion and spirituality are all about *me* and *my* concerns, *my* needs, *my* anxieties, and *my* need to improve *my*self. Rarely are we told that "we discover ourselves in the universe, and the universe discovers itself in us."[10]

Sufi teacher and author Llewellyn Vaughn-Lee calls us back to an *eco*-spiritual perspective:

The Earth is calling to us to realize its essential unity—that She is not a resource to be exploited but a living being crying out for our attention. We are needed to help life to awaken from a dream that is destroying it. But if we are to live the real potential of our spiritual practice, we need to break free from the focus on our own individual journey. We need to reclaim the simple truth that spiritual life is not solely about ourselves, and open to a larger, all-embracing vision. If spiritual life is not about the whole, it has lost its true nature; it has instead been subverted by the ego and its patterns of self-concern. Everything that has been created is in service to life, to the real purpose of creation. This belongs to the "Original Instructions" that were given to the earliest wisdom keepers. We are not separate from each other or from the Earth, and we need to recognize how our individual spiritual journey, our praise and thanksgiving, are part of life's sacred purpose and can nourish life in different ways.[11]

INTERBEING

Even before the Beatles sang, "I am he as you are he as you are me and we are all together,"

Zen master Thich Nhat Hahn introduced the word "Interbeing," which simply means that "Everything relies on everything else in the cosmos in order to manifest—whether a star, a cloud, a flower, a tree, or you and me."[12] We are intimately connected with all that is, in a vast and eternal web of life.

The beloved naturalist, author, and ecologist John Muir describes his "research method," which was profoundly embedded in Interbeing:

> This was my method of study. I drifted about from rock to rock, from stream to stream, from grove to grove. . . . When I discovered a new plant, I sat down beside it for a minute or day, to make its acquaintance and try to hear what it had to say. . . . I asked the boulders I met, whence they came from and whither they were going.[13]

The majority of earthlings in the second decade of the twenty-first century are profoundly estranged from Earth. As climate chaos intensifies and erupts in myriad disruptive events, a spirituality of Earth of the variety that our indigenous ancestors cherished is desperately needed among humans. In fact, humans have no hope of surviving without living with an indigenous sensibility. Embracing intimacy with Earth will not spare us from the natural consequences of our disconnection with Earth, but as we navigate climate chaos, our relationship with the web of life will inevitably deepen as we commit to living in the sacred and allowing the sacred to live in us.

Much like Buddhist teacher Thich Nhat Hahn articulates the notion of Interbeing, John Philip Newell encourages us to find the

> heart of the Earth within our own hearts:
> At the heart of our being and at the heart of all being is the beat of the divine. We do not have to invoke or summon

it from afar. It is here and now, always here, always now. The invitation is simply to awaken to the sacred, to open to it, and in knowing it deep within us to know that we are part of it, and in being part of it to know also that we are part of one another and of everything in the cosmos, the sacred interrelationship of all being. All we have to do is let the very heart of the earth beat within us.[14]

FIERCE PRACTICES

These practices are more effective when we make time to journal and quietly reflect on them without interruption.

- We have all created a false division in our minds between "the sacred" and the Earth. How did that happen for you?
- How are you physically reconnecting with the Earth and healing that division?
- Take time to contemplate the following quote which was stated above by John Muir:

This was my method of study. I drifted about from rock to rock, from stream to stream, from grove to grove. . . . When I discovered a new plant, I sat down beside it for a minute or day, to make its acquaintance and try to hear what it had to say. . . . I asked the boulders I met, whence they came from and whither they were going.

He is describing experiences of intimacy with Earth. Have you experienced this kind of intimacy with the natural world? What was that like for you? If you have not had such an experience, take time to connect with Earth in this way.

CHAPTER 15

THE LIMITS OF THE RATIONAL MIND AND THE HUMAN EGO

Wisdom is a way of knowing that goes beyond one's mind, one's rational understanding, and embraces the whole of a person: mind, heart, and body. —Cynthia Bourgeault, *The Wisdom Way of Knowing*[1]

Seeing the world as separate from ourselves has become the prevailing and institutionalized worldview of the 'academy,' a viewpoint that takes the heart, soul, and magic out of the world, reducing it to the dead, inanimate, insensate domain. In this viewpoint, the universe is mechanized and the heavens secularized. —Paul Levy, *The Quantum Revelation*[2]

Postmodernism ends up with what some call reductionism. We can no longer start from the top and find universal meaning reflected through all of creation. Everything is disconnected, standing on its own, unable to validate itself apart from itself. Everything is diminished and demystified. So, the best we can normally do is take the lowest level that we can control and understand and move up from there—if we can move up at all.

*The language of the reductionist often begins with "only" or
"just," with suspicion and cynicism. This language will determine
ahead of time how much we can see.* —Richard Rohr[3]

After centuries of theological domination by the transcendentally fixated Christian church and following the horrors of Europe's Black Death, a handful of luminaries and researchers began investigating the realities and relationships of the material world, culminating in the Scientific Revolution. While this revolution delivered much of humanity from a purely theological and superstitious worldview, it was also, as Paul Levy writes, "the onset of a particular form of madness."[4]

An essential feature of this madness, says Levy, was "the severing between the subject and object, the observer and the observed, as if the scientific imagination thought that in its intellectual examination of the world, it wasn't part of, participating in, or thereby affecting that which it was investigating."[5] This led to seeing the cosmos as a machine and ourselves as smaller machines within it. As a result, the temptation after centuries of ecclesiastical domination to believe that humans could control the cosmic machine became irresistible.

Lothar Schafer, quantum chemist and Distinguished Professor of Chemistry at the University of Arkansas, argues that, "We have a need to be in touch with the wholeness, and there is a price to be paid when the need is neglected." He quotes psychotherapist Hanne Seemann who says, "My experiences from psychosomatic therapy have taught me that human beings who reside exclusively in the material and rational domain, will sooner or later develop psychosomatic irregularities, because their souls cannot bear this.'"[6]

Nothing could have been more diametrically opposed to

the worldview of traditional indigenous peoples than to "reside exclusively in the material and rational domain" since their life purpose was to live in conscious relationship with the cosmos. Yet it was not until the late nineteenth century that some scientists began exploring quantum physics and in the process, its resonance with what indigenous and other wisdom traditions had known all along: *That everyone and everything is inextricably connected.* On the one hand, our species' capacity to think is extraordinary, yet physicist David Bohm said of thinking, "It has the appearance of independent existence, but that appearance is merely the result of an abstraction of our thoughts." More specifically, he was referring to the illusion of imagining the world to exist separately from ourselves.[7]

When one reads the founding fathers of quantum physics, one hears the resonance of the quantum perspective with the indigenous perspective. For example, David Bohm writes about the "inseparability of the materialistic and spiritualistic views." Physicist John Archibald Wheeler, echoing Thich Nhat Hahn's notion of Interbeing, said, "I think of divinity as being present everywhere," and the late Carl Sagan declared that "Science is not only compatible with spirituality; it is a profound *source* of spirituality."[8]

WISDOM VS. KNOWLEDGE

While we rightfully remain in awe of our capacity to reason and acquire knowledge, it is essential to notice that both are functions of the human ego. However, the ego has little interest in consciousness. In fact, consciousness is not acquired; it simply is. Moreover, unlike the ego, consciousness has the capacity to expand exponentially beyond the margins of the ego. The ego is an instrument of survival, and that which exceeds the limits of the ego potentially threatens its survival.

In indigenous cultures, consciousness and Interbeing are values more highly prized and practical than ego proficiency. Conversely, in industrial cultures where ego performance is more highly valued, when we enter the field of the unknown, the uncertain, the mysterious, the liminal, the ego grows increasingly threatened. These fields challenge the limits of the ego which leaves it feeling vulnerable and unprotected.

Alongside the theological worldview that became entrenched in Western culture prior to the Scientific Revolution, myriad nature-based, mystical wisdom traditions of ancient origin flourished and deepened. Occasionally, more eclectic Christians such as Meister Eckhart, Hildegard of Bingen, Jacob Boehme, Julian of Norwich, and Hadewijch of Antwerp, integrated wisdom teachings into their Christian experience and teaching.

Episcopal priest and student of G.I. Gurdjieff, Cynthia Bourgeault, defines wisdom as "a way of knowing that goes beyond one's mind, one's rational understanding, and embraces the whole of a person: mind, heart, and body."[9] She argues that Descartes' *Cogito Ergo Sum* created a vicious circle: "The process of thinking intensifies our identification of ourselves with the thinker and makes us more and more dependent on thinking as the way of maintaining our sense of identity."[10]

As I work with people who seek coaching in the midst of our predicament, I often ask: What do you believe this crisis is asking of you? The question comes as a surprise to many who never considered that a crisis could be asking a question, let alone asking anything from them personally. One thing I know that it is *not* asking of us is more rational thinking. Obviously, we need to be able to think in order to make day-to-day decisions and respond to our predicament, but rational thinking alone without the wisdom trajectory that embraces mind, heart, and body really is like the proverbial dog chasing its own tail. Moreover, it has gotten us precisely where we are—unfathomably but unalterably confronted with potential extinction.

THE PRACTICE OF AWE AND WONDER

While the words "awe" and "wonder" are not technically synonyms, I am using them as such because I believe that a crucial aspect of the wisdom tradition is the willingness to experience them, not instead of, but alongside our commitment to reason and logic. Helen De Cruz, Chair of Humanities and Philosophy at St. Louis University, examines the role of awe and wonder in scientific practice. In her scientific paper, "Awe and Wonder in Scientific Practice: Implications for the Relationship Between Science and Religion," she writes that:

> I argue that awe and wonder play a crucial role in scientific discovery. They focus our attention on the natural world, encourage open-mindedness, diminish the self (particularly feelings of self-importance), help to accord value to the objects that are being studied, and provide a mode of understanding in the absence of full knowledge... The awe some scientists experience can be regarded as a form of non-theistic spirituality, which is neither a reductive naturalism nor theism.[11]

Notable quantum scientists such as Bohm, Heisenberg, Planck, Schrodinger, and Einstein wrote generously of the awe they experienced in relation to their discoveries. More recent scientists such as Carl Sagan and Neil de Grasse Tyson have unashamedly and profusely written of their awe of the universe.

It is, in fact, through the experience of awe and wonder that so many of the champions of the natural world such as John Muir, Edward Abbey, Jane Goodall, Thomas Berry, Teilhard de Chardin, and Rachel Carson have become passionate defenders of it. In Carson's words:

> What is the value of preserving and strengthening this sense of awe and wonder, this recognition of something beyond the boundaries of human existence? ... Those who dwell, as scientists or laymen, among the beauties and mysteries of the earth, are never alone or weary of life. Whatever the vexations or concerns of their personal lives, their thoughts can find paths that lead to inner contentment and to renewed excitement in living. Those who contemplate the beauty of the earth find reserves of strength that will endure as long as life lasts.[12]

Experiences of awe and wonder are not specifically spiritual ones, but they stir the soul to ask questions of meaning and purpose.

"SOUL" IN THE WISDOM TRADITION

Cogito ergo sum limits our way of knowing exclusively to the rational mind and ego and eliminates the heart and body as instruments of knowledge. The wisdom or mystical way of knowing is far more comprehensive.

Carl Jung included the soul in his research and repeatedly reminded us that the Greek word *psyche* in English means *soul*. For Jung, this was not a religious term, but another name for the Self (with a capital "S") as differentiated from the self as defined by the ego. Becoming whole or individuated for Jung was a process by which the individual develops an intimate relationship with the Self and experiences themselves as defined primarily by the soul rather than the ego. All wisdom traditions nurture this evolutionary journey.

The Christian West, and later, the industrial civilization born from the Scientific Revolution was estranged from the Self, from Earth, and from the web of life. It could only deploy its perspicacity on behalf of the ego and the rational mind. Consequently, knowledge devoid of soul has driven us to the precarious boulders onto which our civilization has ship-wrecked.

In the words of author and social critic Chris Hedges:

> Cultures that do not recognize that human life and the natural world have a sacred dimension, an intrinsic value beyond monetary value, cannibalize themselves until they die. They ruthlessly exploit the natural world and the members of their society in the name of progress until exhaustion or collapse, blind to the fury of their own self-destruction.[13]

Similarly, Zachary Stein offers a direct challenge to those who exclusively embrace the rational mind in a time of climate chaos and societal collapse. He speaks of liminal space or living between worlds—the world of before and the world of after the unprecedented:

> For those identifying as rationalists and scientists, yes, this is why you have been researching, thinking, and "working towards your optimized self." This is a crisis of science and medicine, of economics and game theory—it is a situation in which reason must prevail. But it is also a situation that cannot be handled by reason alone. Consider always the thoughts of the heart, which signal to us at the limits of any

and all models. We do not face a problem that can be solved from any single paradigmatic angle, nor is there any way to ever know everything needed to act with rational certainty. Rational self-interest is the wrong logic, especially in the domains of science where the pandemic has sparked inter-elite competitions for prestige, funding, and claims to legitimacy as the arbiter of truth. Yet what we actually have here is an opportunity to begin to do a new kind of science, where incentives can be realigned in light of the realities encountered in the liminal.[14]

THE CRISIS ASKS A QUESTION

To each of us, our global predicament poses a question: Who do you choose to be as the ship sinks—as the forests burn, as the glaciers melt, as sea levels rise, and as millions of species become extinct? Is *cogito ergo sum* still enough for you? Or do you long to declare: *I feel, I dream, I love, I dance. Therefore, I am.*

FIERCE PRACTICES

These practices are more effective when we make time to journal and quietly reflect on them without interruption.

- What is our global predicament with its vast array of crises asking of you?
- When did you last feel awe or wonder? What was that experience like?
- Change the statement, "I think, therefore I am" into one that more accurately describes you today.

CHAPTER 16
EVOLVE AND DIE: BECOMING A STUDENT OF ENDINGS

Dying wise is a moral obligation. Dying well is not a matter of enlightened self-interest or personal preference. If you can begin to see how dying badly poisons the social, political, professional, and personal discourse about the purpose and meaning of health care and social welfare and being born and dying, if you get a glimpse of how the concentric circles of mayhem and spell casting attending a bad death do not end with that death but actually accelerate and deepen and turn into best practice manuals and family mythologies that have generations of unintended consequences, then you can know each death properly as another chance to die well and to learn the adult mystery of deep living in the face of what often seems to rob life of its depth. Dying well must become an obligation that living people and dying people owe to each other and to those to come. —Stephen Jenkinson[1]

And we are not to live forever but to die well. —Cynthia Bourgeault[2]

Dying is the quintessential spiritual teacher and experience. —
Kathleen Dowling Singh[3]

I n the early days of the collapse-awareness movement,
one often heard the slogan, "Evolve or die." In those days
it was believed that if humans acted quickly enough, we
could save our species from extinction as a result of rampant,
voracious consumption enabled by fossil fuel consumption.
We believed that it was crucial to alter our living arrangements
and do so very quickly in order to survive. However, as long as
we bought into the fantasy of unlimited growth, this would
not be possible, and in order to buy out of the fantasy, we
would need to mentally and emotionally evolve beyond our
infantilized impulses to endlessly consume the planet's
resources.

We watched the documentary *The End of Suburbia*[4] and
shared it with our friends. We took permaculture courses and
moved into intentional communities. Spiritual teachers and
groups, along with eco-psychology classes, proliferated as the
"collapse" theme became viral. As the second decade of the
twenty-first century progressed, "unprecedented" became a
new mantra while science revealed to us how catastrophic our
prognosis would be in the face of climate events that we could
never have imagined.

Humans tended to respond in one of three ways to our
predicament: Denial, Doom, or Deep Adaptation.

The Denial folks, at that time and today still in the majority, minimized the severity of climate chaos and either refused
to think about it or took their vows with the "technology will
save us" gurus. The prevailing mantra of the Doom crowd,
"We're Fucked," focused on the "doomiest" climate science
and its purveyors around whom cults of personality rapidly
erupted. In 2018 Jem Bendell published his paper, "Deep Adap-

tation: A Map for Navigating Climate Tragedy,"[5] and an entire Deep Adaptation movement sprang up—people attempting to live into the global predicament, aspiring to navigate it by holding the tension of opposites.

What was common to all three groups, as well as the entire human species, was and is that all of us are inevitably going to die. Denial and techno-obsessed folks would probably respond to this declaration by saying, "Yes, I'm going to die, but not today." Doomers are unlikely to stop declaring to themselves, and to anyone who will listen, that they are probably going to die in five years or six months or tomorrow. Deep Adapters, on the other hand, would be likely to create or attend a "Die Wise" workshop on one weekend and a "Joy of Living" workshop the next.

DON'T WORRY ABOUT DEATH

In the immortal words of Zen master Kodo Sawaki: *You're worried about death? Don't worry—you'll die for sure.*[6]

Dark humor aside, there is a reason why, in recent years, more humans have been referring to the climate crisis as an *existential crisis*. The challenge is no longer "evolve or die"—as if evolution could prevent death, but rather evolve *and* die. The challenges now are how to confront the inevitability of death and die wisely.

So what does dying well look like then? As Jenkinson emphasizes, "It's not governed by how much pain we're in or how much fear we have or don't have. Those elements are expected to be there. The real honorable dying is the one determined by how we respond to the pain and to the grief and to the utter lack of shared vocabulary and language of the imagination that we can bring to bear upon this momentous and mysterious life event."[7]

In *Die Wise*, Jenkinson states that, "In a culture without much real ceremony, that doesn't tolerate endings of any kind, it's a necessary and proper thing that all of us learn about dying and about death. We must learn how to care for the dying people in our midst, and how to die when it is our turn, well before the time of being tested...comes. This teaching is for people who will die, who are dying, and who love or care for those who will die. It is for those who wish to live deeply and to die well. It teaches the dying time as a place to learn our humanity and the noble, courageous skills of village-making for those we will not live to meet. Chief among these are the willingness to remember sorrow, to start with cultural poverty, to grieve together, and to gather the dead into your village."[8]

We can begin the process of dying wisely here and now by becoming apprentices of sorrow and committing to the work of conscious grieving. Anyone who consents to the sacred work of grieving enters a territory that has never been fully explored or mined in industrial civilization, and it will never "trend" on social media. We lack not only support but even words for our experiences. To die wisely is to enter the terrain of death *now* with all its strangeness and uncertainty and vulnerability. Along the journey, we find and make meaning because we commit to living deeply and embodying the truer, essential definition of *cata-strophe*—making many descents into the depths of the soul, not alone, but "braided together" with our allies. This is what our living in this time has to do with our dying in this time; preparing to die wise can only enhance our aliveness as we evolve *and* die.

What is more, dying wise is about much more than physical death. In fact, in the wisdom traditions, we die wisely every time we defer to the authentic Self and question or challenge or deny the wishes of the ego.

The practice of dying wise will never be welcomed by our

own ego or the egos of the masses. Dying wisely requires deep letting go—deep surrender to the rationally unknown. In general, the ego deplores any lack of control, let alone the conscious act of surrender. For the ego, surrender means "giving up," whereas for the deeper Self, surrender means "giving over." When we give over our plans, our control, and our best strategies, we have agency but not administration. Dying wise or dying with wisdom, not necessarily knowledge, opens us to something greater—vaster, more expansive, more relational, more transformative. For this reason, people often report that in the final moments of dying, they feel more alive than they have ever felt.

As Cynthia Bourgeault explains, surrender

...denotes the passage from the smaller or acorn self into the greater or oak tree Self brought about through this act of letting go. The word surrender itself means to 'hand oneself over' or 'entrust oneself.' It is not about outer capitulation but about inner opening. It is always voluntary, and rather than an act of weakness, it is always an act of strength.[9]

FIERCE PRACTICES

These practices are more effective when we make time to journal and quietly reflect on them without interruption.

- What do "dying wise" or "dying wisely" mean to you? Both terms are related but each means something different from the other.
- How do you feel about your own death?
- What actions have you taken to prepare for your physical death?

- What do you feel when you encounter the word "surrender"?
- Think about a time when you surrendered or "gave over" a situation that you could not control or repair? What happened? How did it feel to surrender?

CHAPTER 17
THE AUDACITY OF JOY

Joy is inexpressibly more than happiness. Happiness befalls people; happiness is fate, while people cause joy to bloom inside themselves. Joy is plainly a good season for the heart; joy is the ultimate achievement of which human beings are capable. — Rainer Maria Rilke[1]

My friends, do not lose heart. We were made for these times...One of the most calming and powerful actions you can do to intervene in a stormy world is to stand up and show your soul. Soul on deck shines like gold in dark times. The light of the soul throws sparks, can send up flares, builds signal fires, causes proper matters to catch fire. To display the lantern of soul in shadowy times like these—to be fierce and to show mercy toward others; both are acts of immense bravery and greatest necessity. —Clarissa Pinkola Estes[2]

H ow dare we speak of joy as our planet, our institutions, and our social structures unravel? How dare I speak of joy in a time when deniers, doomers, and deep adapters struggle with fear, anger, sorrow, anxiety, depression, and a cloud of meaninglessness engulfs our species as we confront, consciously or unconsciously, our potential extinction?

My audacity is informed not by external circumstances but by the clear distinction I make between *happiness* and *joy*.

If we examine the etymology of the word *happiness*, we notice that it is related to other words like *happen, haphazard,* and *happenstance*. That is because the root prefix, *hap*, pertains to fortune or chance. Sometimes we are fortunate enough to be happy, and at other times, we are, unfortunately, *un*-happy. Happiness is circumstantial. If I win the lottery or buy a new outfit or someone throws a birthday party for me, I feel happy. But my happiness is always time-limited and always dependent on what happens in my external world.

So is the "pursuit of happiness" a worthwhile enterprise? For many, the pursuit of happiness never ends. It defines who they are. If they have the means, they can keep it going until the expiration date—the day of their death. If one does not have the means, then one is limited to how much happiness one can pursue, and happiness is reduced to moments instead of a lifetime. Eventually, we run out of those moments and then...?

Perhaps, as author and social critic Barbara Ehrenreich suggests, "In our focus on the nebulous goal of 'happiness,' we seem to have forgotten the far more acute and searing possibility of joy."[3]

In summary, joy and happiness are radically distinct experiences. Happiness is the low-hanging fruit relentlessly available at a moment's notice. However, authentic joy, radical joy, requires a price—the willingness to become conscious and live a life driven by those two questions that will not vanish: *Who do I want to be? What did I come here to do?*

Victor Frankl spoke of "tragic optimism." By this he meant not only making the best of whatever situation one might be in, but also turning suffering into a human achievement and accomplishment; deriving from the guilt that might arise the opportunity to change oneself for the better; deriving from the transitoriness of life an incentive to take responsible action.

Like Carl Jung, Frankl was committed to holding the tension of opposites such as "tragedy" and "optimism." Ultimately, profound suffering not only produces the capacity to hold these opposites, but it also actually compels us to do so. And if we can hold the opposites, our suffering often transforms. Moreover, if we do not become overwhelmed by the suffering, which is no easy task, it is possible to notice within it aspects of beauty, grace, irony, and sometimes even a bit of humor.

Pursuing happiness is an effortless endeavor because it asks nothing of us. After all, it is entirely about what *we* are asking from life. However, cultivating authentic joy requires courage because it asks everything *from us*. Indeed, as Richard Rohr notes in his 2011 book *Falling Upward*, many mystics embraced a kind of *tragic optimism* because of their suffering. One example is John of the Cross, who wrote of "luminous darkness" which "...explains the simultaneous coexistence of deep suffering and intense joy in the saints, which would be impossible for most of us to even imagine."[4]

Rohr speaks of a "bright sadness" among the mystics and others who have allowed suffering to instruct them, and he notes that most individuals have a greater capacity to hold these opposites in the second half of life. While this is typical for most inhabitants of Western culture, it is certainly possible for some individuals to hold "bright sadness" or tragic optimism in the first half of life.

When we understand the profound differences between happiness and joy, the distinction becomes palpable in the presence of individuals who are pursuing happiness and those who possess tragic optimism. The "happy" individual is usually content with superficial conversation and usually resists the exploration of issues in depth. Often their thoughts move rapidly from one thing to another, and their demeanor resembles a swimmer ticking off laps as opposed to the joyful individual who may resemble a scuba diver combing the depths. Happy people tend to be preoccupied with accumulating possessions, polishing their status, and being accepted. Whereas the joyful person may be content with time alone in silence, the happiness seeker is usually given to distraction and staying busy. These observations are not intended as judgments but rather as snapshots of the distinction in perception and motivation in the pursuit of happiness versus the cultivation of joy.

Carl Jung was even more rigorous in his assessment of the pursuit of happiness, describing it as:

> The most elusive of intangibles! Be that as it may, one thing is certain: there are as many nights as days, and the one is just as long as the other in the year's course. Even a happy life cannot be without a measure of darkness, and the word "happy" would lose its meaning if it were not balanced by sadness. Of course it is understandable that we seek happiness and avoid unlucky and disagreeable chances, despite the fact that reason teaches us that such an attitude is not reasonable because it defeats its own ends—*the more you deliberately seek happiness the more sure you are not to find it.*[5]

In a happiness-addicted culture, it is crucial to notice the stark contrast between hoping for happiness and the conscious cultivation of joy as a result of metabolizing meaning.

Recall the words above from Jeremy Lent:

> When we are disconnected from things, when things lose their meaning, we feel bad. When a new pattern comes together, we feel good.

Recall also the words of Comanche activist La Donna Harris, who emphasized the four central values of indigenous people around the world: *Relationship, Responsibility, Reciprocity, Redistribution.*

Remember the interconnectedness of Indra's net and the African principle of Ubuntu: *I am because you are; you are because I am.*

In consciously living our Interbeing, we taste and savor joy, whether for a nanosecond or a lifetime.

In a world battered by climate catastrophe and collapsing systems, we are being asked to enlist as spiritual warriors who seek neither happiness nor hope—who are willing to evolve *and* die. Navigating the landscape through our tragic optimism, we move in the world, committed to our apprenticeship with sorrow—and with joy—bodhisattvas who are repeatedly smitten by the inexplicable beauty of a morning sunrise, the tender patience of the mother robin building her nest, the heart-melting, wizened geography etched in the face of the homeless man on the corner, the suffering that we eased because we were willing to engage in a newfound willingness to be fully present with another human being.

The spiritual warrior's training never ends, and it has led us to this moment. We are perfectly free to desert the ranks, even now, but desertion is a joyless path. We're being asked to live fiercely and show mercy, willingly embracing a journey of "luminous darkness" where deep sorrow and intense joy travel together and need each other.

FIERCE PRACTICES

These practices are more effective when we make time to journal and quietly reflect on them without interruption.

- What is it like for you to experience happiness? What is it like for you to experience joy?
- When did you last feel joy? What was it like?
- Have you ever had the experience of feeling joy amid a painful event or mood?
- Are you ever aware of feeling "tragic optimism" or a "luminous darkness"?
- What is your experience of Interbeing—being part of Indra's net?

CHAPTER 18
AT HOME AS A REFUGEE

The practice of doing our inner work is about wakening our souls and tuning in to the wisdom and gifts that abide within us. Our souls remember our dignity and worth—not over and above someone else. Not in spite of someone else. Not in comparison to anyone else. Our soul is that aspect of ourselves that always remembers our ultimate significance and our connection to the vastness of the cosmos. Our soul is in touch with our inherent somebodiness, and the inherent somebodiness of others. — Unitarian Universalist Association[1]

People will do anything, no matter how absurd, in order to avoid facing their own souls. —Carl Jung[2]

One world is now gone and a new one has yet to emerge; we are now at the beginning of the beginning. —Zachary Stein, *Covid 19: A War Broke Out in Heave*[3]

In the years 2017-2020, wildfires ravaged the West Coast of the United States, destroying homes and businesses on an unprecedented scale. During those years I encountered numerous Americans who had decided to leave the country to reside in other parts of the world. Subsequently, the United States was battered with floods and tornadoes, and countless individuals and families who lacked the means to emigrate were left temporarily or permanently homeless. Meanwhile, countless others who were not directly affected by disasters began quietly planning their departure to other regions domestically or internationally.

As climate-related disasters proliferated worldwide, it became increasingly and painfully obvious that no region was immune to climate catastrophe. The release of the brilliant movie *Nomadland* in 2020 motivated some to buy vans or motorhomes, downsize, and live simpler and more mobile lifestyles in the face of climate uncertainty. If they were healthy and fit enough to pick up temporary jobs along the way, so much the better. Others simply lived on the road, depending on automatic deposits of Social Security checks into their bank accounts.

In February 2022, Russia attacked and invaded its neighbor, Ukraine, sending hundreds of thousands, if not millions of refugees out of the country to other locations in Eastern Europe such as Romania, Poland, Lithuania, Hungary, and Moldova. Within hours or even minutes, millions of Ukrainians became homeless. As of this writing, we do not know how many more Ukrainians will become refugees, nor if or when Russia's aggression will extend into other countries.

In 2022, humans are on the move in response to wars and an uncertain, volatile, and roiling environment. As a result of climate disasters, for the first time in their lives a significant number of white, middle-class Americans have tasted the wrenching reality that millions of poor people and people of color have always known: Having a home is dependent on factors that are only tenuously under one's control. In the twenty-first century, *what* home is and *where* home is are being constantly redefined by climate catastrophe.

Meanwhile, climate refugees pour into the United States from Central America, where unimaginable violence, poverty, and climate chaos are making parts of that region nearly uninhabitable. Globally, the situation is dire, according to *The Guardian*: By 2050, Sub-Saharan Africa could see as many as 86 million internal climate migrants; East Asia and the Pacific, 49 million; South Asia, 40 million; North Africa, 19 million; Latin America, 17 million; and Eastern Europe and Central Asia, 5 million. "Lack of resilience will lead to worsening food insecurity and competition over resources, increasing civil unrest and mass displacement," the report said.[4]

LIMINAL SPACE

The website *Liminal Space* notes that the word *liminal* comes from the Latin word 'limen,' meaning threshold—any point or place of entering or beginning. A liminal space is the time between the 'what was' and the 'next.' It is a place of transition, a season of waiting and not knowing. Liminal space is where all transformation takes place, if we learn to wait and let it form us.

Richard Rohr describes this space as a place where:

We are betwixt and between the familiar and the completely unknown. There alone is our old world left behind, while we are not yet sure of the new existence. That's a good space where genuine newness can begin. Get there often and stay as long as you can by whatever means possible...This is the sacred space where the old world is able to fall apart, and a bigger world is revealed. If we don't encounter liminal space in our lives, we start idealizing normalcy.[5]

These thresholds of waiting and not knowing our "next" are inevitable, and most are incredibly disruptive. Whatever the change, it's a seismic shift, and the future seems uncertain.

When we are facing major change, most of us, if we're honest, don't know who to become or how to navigate ahead. However, we often miss the real potential of "in-between" places because we either stand paralyzed or we flee quickly in order to avoid the discomfort.

In the chapter above on "Uncertainty," I did not use the term *liminal space*, but when we are working to cope with uncertainty, we *are* in liminal space. While it is uncomfortable to stand on a threshold and not know what is next, we can approach it boldly, hold the tension of opposites, be open to the support of others, and eventually move forward.

Zachary Stein astutely comments on the liminal:

In the liminal, there are dangers involving true existential threats, as well as opportunities for fundamentally good repatternings of basic social structures and cultural realties. So much is in play as we navigate through the liminal: infrastructure, medical science, educational systems, economics, and politics are all simultaneously in flux. But as I understand it from my perspective as a psychologist, philosopher, and educator, the risks and opportunities in the realms of human development are not being seen clearly enough.

Who are you becoming?

Who are "we" becoming?

What are the images that dominate our reflections and rumination?

How do we know who we are when "our world" falls apart?

What does it mean to be a person living in a time between worlds?

When the world around someone comes apart, they are placed in a situation where identity transformation becomes necessary. There is an opening into which images and thoughts of all kinds flood the person, when archetypal ideals and horrors are no longer held at bay by the normalcy and routines of the world.[6]

Being in liminal space offers an extraordinary opportunity to contemplate those two familiar questions: *Who do I want to be? What did I come here to do?*

MY INTERNAL ADDRESS

Many of us have become or will become climate or geopolitical refugees as we are exiled by nature or wars into different living arrangements in distant locations—an inevitability that is traumatic at worst and disorienting at best. Regardless of how nomadic we become or conversely, how ensconced in Earth's embrace we may feel, humans, like other animals, require a sense of home—a place of respite and belonging where we can commune with other humans.

It therefore becomes all the more urgent for humans to develop and nurture an internal sense of home as we find ourselves uprooted and unmoored by climate chaos and myriad global disruptions

And so we return again to the red thread that continues to

run through this book and all that I have ever written about our global predicament, namely: *Why and how must we do the inner work that our dire, daunting global predicament is demanding of us?*

Perhaps nothing in current time is more momentous than defining what "home" means to us and creating and tending our home in the *inner* world. In a situation where one has lost one's home and possessions, where remaining in a region that has been our home is no longer possible, and where one can no longer define oneself by where and how one lives, it is crucial to have an inner home to "return to"—a home that does not depend on external circumstances but abides, whatever those circumstances may be.

One reason I began this book with a chapter entitled "Emotions Are Not Enemies" is that developing a relationship with our emotions is a useful practice to begin discovering our inner home. Additionally, a deep exploration of what matters most to us is akin to recognizing that our inner home has a solid foundation. What we feel and what has meaning for us are vital aspects of an inner architecture that remains, no matter where we are in the world.

Although our internal and external homes are not the same, they are interdependent. We naturally feel safer to explore our inner home when external circumstances are peaceful and secure. That is why it is so important to develop our relationship with it before our external world becomes so turbulent that we feel permanently and appallingly unmoored.

One of the most compelling aspects in tending our internal home is to recognize and feel our grief about the loss of our Earth-home as humanity continues to destroy it. Grief roots us deeply within ourselves, no matter where we may be physically. Wherever and whenever one begins the task of tending one's internal home matters little—the web of grief in our psyches is vast and profound and extends far beyond feeling the loss of our planet. When we grieve with those who are available to support us, we discover that our inner home is not isolated, but has "neighbors" who are tending their inner homes alongside us.

As we tend our internal home, it becomes more hospitable and more livable. We discover that what is called for is not "remodeling," but fully inhabiting our inner world—a world that will always be there for us, even as our Earth-home is increasingly diminished. Of this, Michael Meade states:

> When the time of collapse and upheaval comes around again, something ancient in us longs to touch the origins of life. No one can prove it, and no one has to believe it, but something in us can return to a still point where our first breath once formed. In that invisible, inner center, life can renew itself, and we can become imbued with a breath of wholeness and thereby connect to our original life potentials again.[7]

Our human-caused planetary emergency is pleading with us to do the inner work of soul- making and soul-tending so that we may encounter our most authentic humanity and utilize it to heal the wounds inflicted by centuries of external-izing, ego-enhancing, self-aggrandizing endeavors. Thus, Joanna Macy speaks of "the greening of the self," that is, the premise that we are not individuals separate from the world. Instead, we are always "co-arising" or co-creating the world, and we cannot escape the consequences of what we do to the environment. Through "greening the self," we develop our innate ecological or indigenous self—the Self stunted by industrial civilization that longs to thrive in intimacy with Earth.

We also long to thrive in intimacy with each other. As author Mark Nepo writes:

> We keep looking for a home though each of us *is* a home. And no matter where we run, we land before each other, thoroughly exposed. This is the purpose of gravity—to wear us down till we realize we are each other. Though we think we're alone, we all meet here. Though we start out trying to climb over each other, we wind up asking to be held. It just takes some of us longer to land here than others. Once worn of our pretense, it's hard to tolerate arrogance. Once humbled, it's hard to withstand a litany of "me." Once burning off the atmosphere of self-interest, there's a tenderness that never goes away. This tenderness is the sonar by which we sense the interior of life. This tenderness is the impulse that frees us. For anything is possible when we let the heart be our skin. The point is to feel whatever comes our way, not conclude it out of its aliveness. The unnerving blessing about being alive is that it can change us forever. I keep discovering that everyone is loveable, magnificent, and flawed.[8]

FIERCE PRACTICES

These practices are more effective when we make time to journal and quietly reflect on them without interruption.

- What comes to mind when you hear the terms, "inner work" or "inner home"?
- How do you resist these ideas?

- What part of you welcomes attending to an inner home?
- Describe the inner work you are already doing. How does it serve you?
- Since reading about grief in earlier chapters, what is your relationship with your grief today?

CHAPTER 19

A CULTURE DECOMPENSATING INTO PSYCHOSIS

Greater than all physical dangers are the tremendous effects of delusional ideas, which are yet denied all reality by our world-blinded consciousness. —Carl Jung[1]

When the world's most powerful nation goes crazy, the consequences are global. And this is nowhere to be seen more clearly than in the absolute silence about the greatest challenge facing the world community in the foreseeable future, namely, climate change. —W.J.T. Mitchell, Editor of *Critical Inquiry*[2]

We're being haunted by a ghost from the future, of civilization ending in climate catastrophe, quake, flood, fire, fascism, stupidity, social breakdown, economic collapse, violence, brutality... and it's beginning to drive a whole lot of us completely out of our minds. —Umair Haque, "This Is What Civilization Ending Feels Like"[3]

I ndividuals struggling with mental illness need treatment in order to prevent the worsening of their disease. Fortunately, in the past one hundred years, healers from a variety of places and professions have discovered techniques for compassionately treating mental illness. As with most physical ailments, mental illness left untreated will exacerbate, not simply vanish. Structures within the psyche that prevent the worsening of the condition give way, and the individual plummets into a psychotic state which prevents them from functioning in the world.

In the same way that individuals decompensate into psychotic states, so do nations and cultures. However, the deterioration of an individual's mental state may be easier to detect than that of a group.

Currently, in the United States, certain groups within the society are attacking those who teach the dark side of American history as well as its positive aspects. Specifically, those attacking a transparent consideration of our history do not want students to learn about the genocide of millions of Native Americans by white colonizers, which enabled the Anglo-American conquest of North America. Nor do they approve teaching the grotesque truth that white Europeans brought countless numbers of Africans to the Americas to live in slavery. Nor do they want to consider themselves accountable for the horrible consequences of slavery even after the Emancipation. In fact, the opponents of a transparent American history reject any teaching that causes anyone to feel uncomfortable.

American historian Timothy Snyder, in his *New York Times* piece, "The War on History Is a War on Democracy," argues that laws restricting the discussion of race in American schools have dire precedents in Europe. "My experience as a historian of mass killing tells me that everything worth knowing is discomfiting; my experience as a teacher tells me that the process is worth it. Trying to shield young people from guilt prevents them from seeing history for what it was and becoming the citizens that they might be. Part of becoming an adult is seeing your life in its broader settings. Only that process enables a sense of responsibility that, in its turn, activates thought about the future."[4]

I am arguing that shielding people from fact is a form of mental illness in itself. We witnessed yet another cultural example of the phenomenon in the 2022 blockbuster movie, *Don't Look Up*. The movie depicts nothing less than an extravaganza of techniques American society uses to ignore or deny the severity of environmental catastrophe. America's snowflake mentality regarding both its history and climate science appalls citizens of numerous other developed nations around the world.

Let us take history, for example. Germany has been teaching its children about the holocaust for decades. In a *New Yorker* article, "What Can We Learn from the Germans about Confronting Our History?" philosopher and Director of the Einstein Forum in Berlin, Susan Neiman, concludes that, "The lesson for Americans—particularly those involved in racial-justice work—is that *Nobody* wants to look at the dark sides of their history. It's like finding out that your parents did something really horrible. There's always going to be resistance. It's normal, and it's something we should expect."

So what made the Germans change? Neiman writes about a number of historical factors, but the most important, in her opinion, was "civil engagement" by the German public, beginning in the nineteen-sixties. A new generation came of age. "They realized that their parents and teachers had been Nazis, or at least complicit in Nazi atrocities, and were outraged," she said. A small and often controversial vanguard insisted on digging up history that older generations had refused to discuss. People called them *Nestbeschmützer*, or "nest-foulers." But the process they set in motion—a process of uncovering the past and talking about it—eventually reverberated throughout German society.[5]

TRAUMA IS ON EVERYONE'S MIND

In her *Salon* article, "Is America Experiencing Mass Psychosis?" Nicole Karlis describes a plethora of distortions spreading virulently in American culture. Among them are the notion that powerful people planned the Covid outbreak; that Presidential election results cannot be trusted; that the Covid vaccines are attempts to debilitate and control populations so that the ruling elite can advance its agenda; that Joe Biden is the illegitimate President of the United States; and that Donald Trump will save America from a cabal of pedophiles who are physically devouring America's children.

As I peruse journals of psychology and mental health, as I speak with therapists and mental health care workers, and as I observe the plethora of online workshop offerings, I am amazed but not surprised by the frequency with which the word *trauma* appears. I am convinced that none of us escapes it consciously or unconsciously. But sadly, I am certain that collective trauma will only intensify as industrial civilization continues to unravel.

In the throes of a deadly global pandemic whose end we may never fully experience in our lifetimes, in the face of countless environmental disasters—past, present, and future, groping our way amid political division such as we have not seen since the Civil War, with talk of an imminent second Civil War, surrounded by racial inequality and its subtle and blatant forms of racism, bombarded as we are with gaslighting and loathsome quantities of lies and disinformation in a culture so dumbed-down that holding an actual book in one's hand and reading it is considered bizarre, mind-raped as we are by gargantuan quantities of social media disinformation, experiencing every aspect of our lives disrupted or about to be—how is anyone not traumatized?

According to the Yale School of Medicine, "Illness, grief, job loss, social isolation, uncertainty, and other pandemic-driven stressors have contributed to an increase in psychological distress on an unusually wide scale. As researchers and clinicians continue to grapple with the psychological fallout from COVID-19, a growing body of literature has examined the prevalence of post-traumatic stress disorder (PTSD) in the general public."[6]

Everyone who has experienced an environmental disaster or has been in close proximity to one carries some form of trauma. Having witnessed the ghastly wildfire driven by hurricane-force winds that occurred in December 2021 along the Front Range of Colorado, I find my own anxiety rising every time I hear the wind blow. Has that been traumatic? Indeed. Am I suffering from PTSD? Probably, but certainly less than anyone who actually lost their home and possessions in the fire.

The mindboggling proliferation of violence in the United States is inevitable given that "American civilians own at least 265million firearms, which gives Americans the highest rate of per capita firearm ownership in the world, with about one gun for every American."[7] As climate catastrophe intensifies, as systems collapse, and as levels of trauma and PTSD escalate, we can expect to witness levels of violence which we may not presently be able to imagine. People buy guns for myriad reasons, but gun owners consistently report that owning a gun or guns "makes them feel safer."[8] While owning a gun protects no one from climate catastrophe, pandemics, or the collapse of systems, many Americans nevertheless "feel safer" owning one. In a recent conversation with a friend, she reported that no sooner had the Covid pandemic erupted in the United States than she received a phone call from her brother, who asked her, "Are you packin'?"

As the culture decompensates into unprecedented dysfunction, we can expect to see increased violence and even more people owning and using guns. Social critic Umair Haque offers a chilling clarification:

> Only one side in America has the guns, and wants to use them...In America, only *one* side has been radicalized into violence and hate... in this day and age, left-wing violence *does not exist*. Not really. Maybe, maybe in parts of Latin America. China's treatment of the Uighurs isn't so much "left-wing" as it is totalitarian. But in America? The idea that there's some kind of left wing—or even center— with guns, that's willing to use them, is laughable. It is simply nonexistent. It isn't there, such a political faction...So the center is impotent, while the left is infantile. The right, meanwhile, has guns, and is willing to use them.[9]

SHADOW WARS

I believe that the war on history is not disconnected from the myriad distortions that now afflict industrially civilized culture. As I argue in my book *Dark Gold: The Human Shadow and the Global Crisis,* the denial of the shadow is replete with consequences. Disowning the disturbing realities of our history has profoundly damaged our psyches because when the shadow is ignored or denied, any possibility of healing it vanishes and only increases the severity of the disease, thus sealing the fate of America as a toxic empire. Speaking of the shadow's capacity to delude us, Jung summarized it most accurately:

> Our much-vaunted reason and our boundlessly overestimated will are sometimes utterly powerless in the face of 'unreal' thoughts.[10]

Jungian analyst Katherine Bainbridge says, "Something's definitely happening, and I think COVID amplified it to a painful point, you could say...It's complicated. From the left's point of view, people that aren't being vaccinated or think the election was rigged are psychotic, right? If you're on the right, you think the left is psychotic and has lost its mind in identity politics. Both sides look at each other and say, 'you've lost your mind.'"[11]

Bainbridge also emphasized the role of myth: "In order to contextualize what's actually happening in America through a Jungian lens, one must consider the role of a central guiding myth...Jung said man cannot live without religion—so you make it up. You can't not have a central myth to live by. He would say maybe in this time that we've lost that—we don't have a collective unifying principle."[12]

Bainbridge notes that with many Americans leaving organized religion in staggering numbers, we see an increase in membership in New Age religions or movements. Others have joined far-right extremist groups such as QAnon. "One is super-dark and apocalyptic, and the other is utopian," she said. "The problem with New Age thinking is that it leaves out the shadow—and then QAnon is obsessed with the shadow."

Joe Kelly, a cult intervention specialist, opines that humans are often drawn to extremism when they are suffering. "If an individual is hurting—financially, on any level, losing a job, having trouble with their mortgage, having trouble feeding themselves—then they're more likely to listen to extremist ideologies and talk about a conspiracy around them that is beyond their control," Kelly said.

Katherine Bainbridge concludes: "We have to find our humanity, and [ask], 'what does it mean to be a human being?' It means that you have to integrate your own darkness, wrestle with your own paradoxes and stop projecting out onto other people the opposite inside of you."[13]

Michael Meade, mythologist and storyteller, is profoundly aware of the painful consequences for humans when we lack a collective myth or meaningful story. In a recent podcast, "Finding Our Way by Falling," Meade echoes the central theme of my work:

The collective situation we are now in is overburdened with conflicts and oppositions, but also subject to sudden changes and extremes of all kinds. With each issue that becomes a source of conflict, we see how fragile life is, how the threads that weave things together can easily unravel. Increasingly, we see how the life maps we have been given do not match the terrains of confusion and places of upheaval we keep falling into. Part of what drives people to extreme beliefs and behaviors is that many of our received ideas and common beliefs turn out to be unequal to the radical events we are witnessing. In the face of radical changes, people not only become disoriented, but can feel a loss of personal identity. This is especially true where people have over-identified with a collective point of view, a national identity or a particular ideology.

An old idea states that creation is the only outcome of conflict that can satisfy the human soul. In that sense, the stability and coherence we most desire involves a deeper connection to our own soul. And our souls require that we find ways to become part of a revisioning of life and a recreation of the world.

Sometimes we must find our way by falling. If we deny or resist the sense of loosening and falling that comes at the end of an era, we not only risk being caught in social or political extremes, we also risk losing our wings and the spirit of our own lives. And we can lose the possibility of becoming more conscious agents of a recreation that is also trying to happen in the midst of all the uncertainty and upheaval that accompany times of change.[14]

I, ME, MINE

Particularly in the United States, but in other nations as well, we see the rebuke and demise of a sense of the common good or "the commons." American hyper-individualism dictates that the functioning of a society is about making personal choices and that those choices supersede the commons. Nothing has illuminated this notion in our culture like the Covid 19 pandemic has. In the early days of the pandemic, people marched in solidarity with healthcare workers and gathered outside their homes every evening to howl and deploy noisemakers to support them. Suddenly, fed by fear and pervasive disinformation, perpetuated by myriad forms of media, as well as a novel anti-intellectualism and contempt for science, the pandemic became a battleground of conspiracy theory and political allegiance. Divergent opinions about the pandemic and vaccination have deepened chasms that already existed, and the result has been an even more dramatic deterioration of the notion of the common good.

Hyper-individualism in any society does not bode well for its inhabitants as they find themselves engulfed in climate meltdown amid increasingly authoritarian political proclivities. As societies become more authoritarian, they tend to become more isolated, individualistic, and paranoid, making all manner of crises much more treacherous to navigate in silos of separation. In fact, a sense of community has never been more imperative, nor has it ever been more difficult to actualize and engage with.

To find our way in a culture cratering into psychosis, we need an internal home as defined above, as well as a collective myth which is developed and lived with allies who comprehend our external predicament and the necessity of intimacy with nature and with the soul so that together, we may revision and recreate the world. As climate chaos intensifies, as our existence on this planet becomes increasingly uncertain, as many of us become refugees while society becomes bewilderingly unstable, divided, and perhaps even more violent, something greater—within us and within nature—must be our ultimate Global Positioning System (GPS).

FIERCE PRACTICES

These practices are more effective when we make time to journal and quietly reflect on them without interruption.

- In what ways have you found yourself caught in culture wars and political divisions?
- How has the global pandemic affected you and your loved ones?
- What events have been most traumatizing for you in the past five years?
- Tonglen Meditation is a Tibetan Buddhist practice for engaging with the world by mindfully opening to its suffering as well as directing love and healing to people and situations who are suffering or are

the cause of suffering. Highly recommended are "Tonglen Meditations" by American Buddhist teacher Pema Chodron. They can be found at YouTube.

- People relate to soul in a variety of ways—through music, art, literature, film, spiritual practices, nature, and more. Describe your relationship with soul. What kinds of experiences deepen your relationship with soul?

PART TWO

PERSEVERING IN AN AUTHORITARIAN WORLD

If you can feel that staying human is worthwhile, even when it can't have any result whatever, you've beaten them. — George Orwell[1]

Aliveness comes down to one thing—consenting to rise, to be dented, impressed, pressed in upon, to rejoin, to open, to ponder, to be where we are in this moment and see what happens, allowing the breath of not knowing to be taken, wanting to see what is there and what is not there. Aliveness springs from our making something of what we experience and receiving what experience makes of us. This is the wonder of the child the New Testament always recommends us to return to, what the philosopher Paul Ricœur calls our "second naiveté". . . . In such a space we allow ourselves to depend on something greater than ourselves, to take what it gives us and respond to it.

This struggle to live all we can in the face of death, illness, loss of relationship, unbearable grief, acts of injus-

tice, is a struggle we share in all our different circumstances of life. . . . In the New Testament words, the pearl of great price is what we sell all we have for the sake of; riches, fame, security [which] do not ensure simple happiness in being, only this precious aliveness. What, then, is that pearl of great price? It is feeling alive and real, vibrantly the aliveness that belongs to each of us. —Ann Belford Ulanov, Jungian Analyst[2]

CHAPTER 20
THE BAD GUYS ARE WINNING

If the 20th century was the story of a slow, uneven struggle, ending with the victory of liberal democracy over other ideologies —communism, fascism, virulent nationalism—the 21st century is, so far, a story of the reverse. —Anne Applebaum, "The Bad Guys Are Winning"[1]

So here we are, in a nation where violent insurrection is being downplayed by half the country and even lawmakers who were hunkered down in the building under attack at the time...This is authoritarianism at its finest. It is fascism, American style. There is no middle ground, no neutral in the face of such things as this... There are many ways to be anti-fascist, and they certainly don't all include pouring into the streets or mixing it up with Nazis... But it does mean taking a stand. It does mean being willing to declare yourself implacably opposed to authoritarianism. —Tim Wise, author and Anti-Racism educator[2]

Argue all you want about the physical world, but Nature is the ultimate arbiter: serving as judge, jury, and executioner. —Neil

133

de Grasse Tyson[3]

Within the past two years as I have published my *Daily News Digest* and various blog posts, some readers have challenged the ink that I have devoted to my warnings regarding the demise of democracy in the twenty-first century. Many argue that America, as well as other Western countries, were never pure democracies, and it is hypocritical to concern ourselves with the current discourse on the topic. Instead, they prefer to focus on climate chaos, asserting that it is a far more ominous threat than the loss of whatever we define democracy to be. At first blush, the argument sounds plausible. After all, doesn't the possibility of an unprecedented extinction event render any conversation about democracy absurd?

On the one hand, climate meltdown could destroy most or all of life on the planet. It obviously has the potential to make Earth uninhabitable. How could any topic of discussion be more momentous? At the same time, however, when we consider that as democracy, or even the appearance of democracy declines, so do nearly all concerns regarding ecosystems and any sense of Interbeing and compassionate care for each other. Autocratic societies eventually lose all interest in even the pretense of caring for the environment and grow increasingly rapacious and avaricious with the natural world. Even now, this is becoming increasingly obvious in terms of climate chaos.

In his 2014 book, *Windfall: The Booming Business of Global Warming*, McKenzie Funk writes that while many might believe that businesses that help to fight or reduce climate change—solar panel manufactures, for example—may be the ones with the most to gain from a changing environment, those looking to reap the benefits of the damage to the Earth will also profit. "There's a lot of money going into genetic modification. Monsanto and Syngenta are a big part of any climate fund's portfolio because they expect they'll do better in a warming world."[4]

In addition to agribusinesses and hedge funds benefiting from environmental damage, Funk says that some governments are also able to generate capital from climate change.

"If you travel to Holland or the Netherlands and you talk to people, there's not a lot of gloom, there's a lot of talking about climate change as an opportunity," says Funk. "For a country that's spent generations preparing for sea level rise, they want to sell that expertise to the world and they're doing so increasingly. There are engineering companies that will build sea walls and storm surge barriers like that for New York City. There are ones that will build you an entire floating city—not just floating homes, but floating parks, floating schools, floating streets. They're beginning to sell that technology everywhere."[5]

In his *Guardian* article, "Climate denial is waning on the right. What's replacing it might be just as scary," Oliver Milman notes that more conservative nations are denying climate chaos less, but preoccupying themselves with climate-induced immigration more obsessively. "'Simply ignoring or disparaging the science isn't the effective political weapon it once was. We are seeing very, very little climate denialism in conversations on the right now,' said Catherine Fieschi, a political analyst...who tracks trends in populist discourse. 'But in place of denial is a growing strain of environmental populism that has attempted to dovetail public alarm over the climate crisis with disdain for ruling elites, longing for a more traditional embrace of nature and kin and calls to banish immigrants behind strong borders.'"[6]

ECO-FASCISM

Patrick Crusius, the Dallas, Texas man accused of killing twenty-three people in a mass shooting at a Walmart in El Paso, Texas, in 2019, wrote: "The environment is getting worse by the year ... So the next logical step is to decrease the number of people in America using resources. If we can get rid of enough people, then our way of life can become more sustainable." The shooting came just a few months after the terrorist massacre of forty-nine people in two mosques in Christchurch in New Zealand, with the perpetrator describing himself as an eco-fascist unhappy about the birthrate of immigrants. What is more, some individuals on the far right believe that nature is a place of savage survival that brings us back to original society and that nature itself is fascist because there is no equality in nature.[7]

As we witnessed with the proto-fascist Trump Administration, the topic of "climate change" rarely arose, and several members of Trump's Cabinet were some of the worst environmental villains on Earth—such as Andrew Wheeler, Secretary of the Environmental Protection Agency, a coal lobbyist who replaced Scott Pruitt who was a climate change denier and a cozy ally of oil and gas companies.

Some of the bad guys that appear to be winning are Russia's Putin, Hungary's Orbán, Poland's Duda, Turkey's Erdogan, the Philippines' Duterte, Brazil's Bolsonaro, India's Modi, Venezuela's Maduro, and Myanmar's military coup. What is beginning to constellate is an Axis of Autocrats who deplore democracy at the same time that the future of what is left of democracy in the United States is beyond precarious as a result of its accelerating trajectory toward total collapse.

While I have been writing this book, Russia, under Vladimir Putin, has invaded Ukraine. It is likely that as of

February 2022, Russia's naked aggression against Ukraine and Eastern Europe has only begun to play out.

Traditionally, leaders of authoritarian regimes have been overwhelmingly male and have preferred hierarchies and top-down leadership over the relational democratic process which they find tedious and time-consuming. Furthermore, as systems teeter and eventually collapse, collaborative leadership and problem-solving have almost always succumbed to authoritarian rule. That has usually proven advantageous for the strongman and provided a false sense of security for the citizenry.

However, this model of the far-right fascist leader is beginning to change, according to journalist Anne Applebaum:

> All of us have in our minds a cartoon image of what an auto-cratic state looks like. There is a bad man at the top. He controls the police. The police threaten the people with violence. There are evil collaborators, and maybe some brave dissidents. But in the 21st Century, that cartoon bears little resemblance to reality. Nowadays, autocracies are run not by one bad guy, but by sophisticated networks composed of kleptocratic financial structures, security services—military, police, paramilitary groups, surveillance—and professional propagandists. The members of these networks are connected not only within a given country, but among many countries. The corrupt, state-controlled companies in one dictatorship do business with corrupt, state-controlled companies in another. The police in one country can arm, equip and train the police in another. The propagandists share resources—the troll farms that promote one dictator's propaganda can also be used to promote the propaganda of another—and themes, pounding home the same messages about the weakness of democracy and the evil of America.[8]

The authoritarian impulse is far too palpable and daunting to minimize. Ranking it less formidable than climate chaos is naïve and myopic. In fact, as the movie *Don't Look Up* emphasized, climate uncertainty offers endless opportunities for corporate capitalists to seize and exploit it for profit and power.

What is more, most Americans appear to be simply incapable of grasping the severity of the authoritarian trajectory. In his *Mother Jones* piece, "The Trump Coup: Maybe We Can't Handle the Truth," editor David Corn cites Jeffrey Engel, President of Southern Methodist University, who recently wrote that, "I actually think the American public is dramatically underplaying how significant and dangerous this is because we cannot process the basic truth of what we are learning about President Trump's efforts—which is we've never had a president before who fundamentally placed his own personal interests above the nation's."[9] Corn therefore concludes: "But Engel's larger point is intriguing: Trump's wickedness may be too immense for the nation to absorb."[10]

We must acknowledge the reality that as we live into climate meltdown, we are likely to be doing so, either directly or indirectly, in the shadow of authoritarian regimes that will be highly motivated to profit from climate chaos.

As the bad guys continue to win and the ecosystems wither, how is it possible to live sanely—even fiercely, vibrantly, and joyfully amid the madness? While there are no easy or effortless answers, history has gifted us with role models who would undoubtedly be honored were we to aspire to following their example.

CHAPTER 21
ROLE MODELS OF JUSTICE AND COURAGE

Those who contemplate the beauty of the earth find reserves of strength that will endure as long as life lasts. There is something infinitely healing in the repeated refrains of nature—the assurance that dawn comes after night, and spring after winter. — Rachel Carson, *Silent Spring*[1]

We drew sustenance and strength from the knowledge that we were part of a greater humanity than our jailers could claim. — Nelson Mandela[2]

Bless you prison, bless you for being in my life. For there, lying upon the rotting prison straw, I came to realize that the object of life is not prosperity as we are made to believe, but the maturity of the human soul. —Aleksandr I. Solzhenitsyn, *The Gulag Archipelago 1918–1956, Vol. II*[3]

I f we are going to live into climate meltdown in an authoritarian world, and if we are to muster the courage within ourselves to champion the wholeness of our ecosystems in the face of corporate, neo-fascist opposition, we need to remind ourselves of the individuals who committed their lives to freedom and justice in the face of oppression, imprisonment, torture, and death. Their example can inspire us when we feel engulfed in despair.

We must first consider that their commitment arose from the deeper Self that transcends the rational mind and human ego. Secondly, we must never shame ourselves if we cannot endure what they endured. We must do what is ours to do, always remembering that we are imperfect human beings motivated by love—love of the sacred, love of the Earth, love of our community, love of justice and compassion.

ENTER THEMIS

In Greek mythology, Themis, whose name means *justice*, was a consort of Zeus and the daughter of Gaia. She is depicted as a beautiful, blindfolded woman holding the scales of justice in one hand and a sword in the other. Her blindfold symbolizes impartiality and fairness as she protects the oppressed and promotes hospitality.[4]

Throughout human history, countless individuals have incarnated the archetype of Themis and in many cases, sacrificed their lives for it. To assist us in reclaiming the principles of Themis and living undaunted in the face of ecological and social injustice, this chapter offers some examples of justice-makers in modern times.

VIKTOR FRANKL

I have mentioned Frankl several times in this book, not because I perceive him as the ultimate example of justice and courage, but because more than most role models of these qualities, he survived his suffering through finding meaning in it. Not to have done so would have guaranteed his death. In *Man's Search for Meaning*, he notes the three ways that we find or make meaning: 1) Actions that are meaningful to us and others, such as service; 2) Experiencing beauty through art and through a loving relationship; 3) Suffering.

While the third is not necessarily in the absence of the first two, within Frankl's frame of thought, suffering became an option through which to find meaning and experience one's values in life in the absence of the other two opportunities.[5]

For Frankl, meaning and joy are inextricably connected. Joy, he believed, results from meaning, not the pursuit of happiness. Therefore, it is possible to experience joy when we are very unhappy but are nevertheless engaged in a meaningful activity. "The experiences of camp life," Frankl said, "show that man does have a choice of action.... Man can preserve a vestige of spiritual freedom, of independence of mind, even in such terrible conditions of psychic and physical stress."[6]

The pivotal issue for Frankl was how we meet our suffering. Even if we have been victimized, do we respond to suffering as a victim or as a vulnerable human being who is willing to open to the meaning inherent in our suffering with agency and awareness?

HANNAH ARENDT

In the summer of 1950, Hannah Arendt wrote: "We can no longer afford to take that which was good in the past and simply call it our heritage, to discard the bad and simply think of it as a dead load which by itself, time will bury in oblivion. The subterranean stream of Western history has finally come to the surface and usurped the dignity of our tradition. This is the reality in which we live. And this is why all efforts to escape from the grimness of the present into nostalgia for a still intact past, or into the anticipated oblivion of a better future, are vain."[7]

In her book, *The Origins of Totalitarianism*, Arendt was reflecting on the roots of the fascist worldview in Germany following World War I. Today, we see the variety of nostalgia to which she refers becoming increasingly ubiquitous in the twenty-first century as nations seem magnetically drawn to authoritarianism—a wistful yearning for a cozy, illusory past in which white people outnumbered people of color, immigrants, and Jews. In the United States, white parents imagine a time when children were not exposed to books that contain topics of racism, misogyny, or diverse sexual orientation. Republican politicians, terrified of diverse ethnicities surpassing the population of Anglo-Americans in the twenty-first century, are conspiring to suppress the non-white vote and manipulate elections to favor whites.

Arendt's most famous works, *The Origins of Totalitarianism* and *The Banality of Evil* articulate her reflections and realizations regarding the proliferation of fascism in the twentieth century. Herself a Jew, she fled Nazi Germany in 1933 and eventually settled in the United States in 1941, where she became an American citizen. Compared with many outspoken anti-fascist contemporaries, she endured minor persecution, but her profound and painful reflections nourished her spirit and inspired millions to study and protest all forms of totalitarianism.

A *Boston Review* article about her opines that "Arendt turned Jewish persecution on its head and demanded Jewish resistance not for the sake of the Jews alone, but for that of the entire modern world.... This idea of responsible world citizenship became key for Arendt. It led her to the passionate conviction that the sovereign state must come to an end, as nationalism in the 20th century had clearly proved itself the enemy of humanity. The state, she thought, should give way to federated commonwealths, each composed of a system of local governments—townships, councils, soviets—within which majorities and minorities would no longer be accorded differential rights. Such a system would facilitate the grassroots practice of direct democracy, whereby 'freedom will consist of political action among equals.' A utopian vision, no doubt, but one held by social revolutionists like the anarchists, who had repeatedly made use of the vision to think hard about what human beings need to feel human."[8]

Arendt's principal gift to the world was her capacity to discern how nations are seduced by authoritarianism and how we can liberate ourselves by contemplating what our deepest humanity requires. She would not have framed her thesis in spiritual terms, but when she is thinking about "what humans need to feel human," she is doing just that.

DIETRICH BONHOEFFER

Bonhoeffer was a German theologian who declared himself a pacifist, but by the late 1930s, he joined a resistance movement to oppose Hitler because he could no longer justify doing nothing. Ultimately, he supported the assassination of Hitler.

To avoid being drafted into the regular Army, Bonhoeffer took a position with German military intelligence (*Abwehr*). There he became part of a resistance cell inside the organization. Bonhoeffer was assigned to travel outside Germany, ostensibly to gather intelligence for the Nazis. Instead, he provided the Allies with information about the activities of the German resistance and tried to enlist allied support for them. (In spy novels, that's known as being a "double agent.") Unfortunately, the Allied powers ignored his requests. In 1943, Bonhoeffer's fellow resisters tried to kill Hitler. They failed. The Gestapo identified Bonhoeffer as part of the plot. They arrested him and sent him to prison.

Earlier, in a widely influential book, *The Cost of Discipleship*, Bonhoeffer had condemned what he called "cheap grace"— accepting God's love without cost. At the same time, he extolled "costly grace"—grace that requires radical obedience, even the willingness to die for one's beliefs, which Bonhoeffer did.

Bonhoeffer was arrested by the Nazis in April, 1943 after it was discovered that he used his government position to help a number of Jews escape to Switzerland.[9]

Journalist Rohit Kumar notes that "Dietrich Bonhoeffer... wondered how a nation that had given the world Gutenberg, Goethe, and Beethoven could possibly have embraced a madman like Hitler? Bonhoeffer thought about it long and hard. Was it a deep, hidden malice against the Jews that had finally surfaced, or had ordinary Germans simply fallen prey to Goebbels's propaganda machinery? Or was it a combination of both?"[10] Writing from his prison cell, Bonhoeffer attributes Germany's ghastly decline to stupidity.

Stupidity is a more dangerous enemy of the good than malice. One may protest against evil...(but) against stupidity we are defenseless. Reasons fall on deaf ears. When facts are irrefutable, they are just pushed aside as inconsequential, as incidental.[11]

Echoing the conclusion of many observers of the United States in 2022, only stupidity permits the rise of totalitarianism and the intellectual defaults that pave the way for tyranny. As I read Bonhoeffer's essay, I am reminded of the current cultural hysteria around teaching accurate American history in public schools, anti-climate science, anti-vaccine disinformation, bizarre QAnon conspiracy theories, and the notion that Donald Trump, not Joe Biden, is President of the United States.

From 1933-1935, Bonhoeffer was given the opportunity to pastor two churches in London. He could have remained there until the end of World War II, but he chose to return to Germany in 1935. Upon arriving back in Germany, Bonhoeffer was asked to direct the seminary for the Confessing Church in Finkenwalde, Germany. By December, Himmler declared all examinations for the Confessing Church invalid, all training there invalid, and all participants liable to arrest. Bonhoeffer then applied to teach at Berlin University, but his authorization to do so was withdrawn in 1936. Bonhoeffer continued traveling abroad from 1937 to 1945, teaching students and mentoring churches. Upon his return to Germany he was arrested and sent to Flossenburg Concentration Camp, where he was hanged on April 9, 1945—only a few weeks before Germany surrendered.

Bonhoeffer was an irrepressible activist who was under Nazi surveillance for years but never faltered. He knew the price of his "discipleship"—his commitment to truth and justice, and ultimately he paid it.

Discipleship is not limited to what you can comprehend—it must transcend all comprehension. Plunge into the deep waters beyond your own comprehension, and I will help you to comprehend even as I do. Bewilderment is the true comprehension. Not to know where you are going is the true knowledge.[12]

I am fascinated by the words, *Bewilderment is the true comprehension. Not to know where you are going is the true knowledge.* Bonhoeffer's words echo Buddhist wisdom and the "unalterable uncertainty" we considered in an earlier chapter. He did not know where he was headed, yet he persevered and became a remarkable inspiration to future generations of individuals who would be compelled to engage in unprecedented soul-searching with regard to their personal values and loyalty to institutions.

SOPHIE SCHOLL

Like Dietrich Bonhoeffer, Sophie Scholl grew up in a Lutheran home in Southwestern Germany, but by the time she became a teenager, Hitler was running the country. Like many young German idealists, Sophie and her older brother Hans supported the National Socialist Party. Like many other youngsters, Hans joined the party's Hitler Youth movement and Sophie joined its sister organization, the League of German Girls. However, the two were ultimately unable to reconcile their own liberal leanings with the politics of the Third Reich. They couldn't help but see the way in which Jewish acquaintances and artists were treated. They began to view the regime through increasingly critical eyes. Their final eye-opener was Hitler's invasion of Poland in 1939.

Hans enrolled in the University of Munich to study medicine, and Sophie followed him there to study biology, although she was a talented painter. Hans' friend, Alexander Schmorell, formed the White Rose Society, which encouraged citizens to resist the Nazi regime, denouncing the murder of Jewish people and demanding an end to the war.

It's not clear why Sophie climbed to the top-floor landing that overlooked the airy atrium of the university's main building and flung a stack of political pamphlets over the balustrade. Most assume she wanted as many students as possible to see them. But, as the papers fluttered down to the ground, she was watched by a caretaker who betrayed her to the Gestapo.

She and her brother were interrogated, and after a show trial, sentenced to death. They refused to betray the rest of the group, but the authorities tracked them down anyway. Within a few months the friends had all been executed.

On the morning that she went to the guillotine, Sophie, aged 21, said:

"Such a fine, sunny day, and I have to go... What does my death matter, if through us, thousands of people are awakened and stirred to action?"

Those words and her bravery are still honored in Germany today, where schools and roads bear her name and that of her brother. [13]

NELSON MANDELA

Mandela was a South African anti-apartheid revolutionary, political leader, and philanthropist who served as the first president of South Africa from 1994 to 1999. He was the country's first black head of state and the first elected in a fully representative democratic election. His government focused on dismantling the legacy of apartheid by tackling institutionalized racism and fostering racial reconciliation. Ideologically an African nationalist and socialist, he served as the president of the African National Congress (ANC) party from 1991 to 1997.

Mandela was imprisoned for 27 years, during which time his mother died and his son was in a fatal car accident. But Mandela was forbidden to attend either funeral. First as a lawyer, then as an activist, and ultimately as a guerrilla leader, Mandela moved towards a collision with state power that would change his own and his country's fate.

The late 1950s and early 1960s were a period of growing tumult in South Africa, as African nationalists, allied with the South African Communist Party, challenged the apartheid state. When protest was met with brute force, the ANC launched an armed struggle with Mandela at its head. He was arrested and charged with treason in 1956. After a trial lasting five years, Mandela was acquitted.

But by then the ANC had been banned, and so Mandela embarked on a secret trip to ask for help from other African nations emerging from colonial rule. However, in 1962 he was arrested and sentenced to five years in jail. Further charges of sabotage led to a life sentence that would see him spend 27 years behind bars.

After the sentencing, there were pro-Mandela demonstrations in Britain as well as a world petition calling for his release, which was handed to the United Nations Secretary General.

Despite a world movement demanding his freedom, Mandela ended up serving his sentence until apartheid ended. He was sentenced to life on June 12, 1964, and released on February 11, 1990. Mandela was jailed initially on Robben

Island, a former leper colony, for 18 years. In 1982 he was moved to Pollsmoor Prison outside Cape Town and later served time at the Victor Verster Prison.

When Mandela was released unconditionally from prison, he walked free with his then-wife, Winnie, and appeared before 50,000 people on the balcony of City Hall and thanked "the millions of my compatriots and those in every corner of the globe who have campaigned tirelessly for my release."[14]

His lasting influence on politics and human rights have meant that his legacy will follow him for years to come. Between his work to end apartheid and his dream of a non-racist South African government, Mandela contributed greatly toward lasting peace in South Africa, as well as the end of many oppressive and racist governmental policies.

Mandela famously said, "A democratic and free society in which all persons live together in harmony and with equal opportunities is an ideal for which I am prepared to die."[15] He did not die a martyr, but he lived his life confronting racism and an authoritarian regime—enduring 27 years in prison, many forms of brutality, and separation from his family and community.

"It is not our diversity which divides us," Mandela said; "it is not our ethnicity, or religion or culture that divides us. Since we have achieved our freedom, there can only be one division amongst us: between those who cherish democracy and those who do not." [16]

ETTY HILLESUM

As a young Jewish writer living in Amsterdam in the 1940s, Etty Hillesum kept diaries about Nazi oppression as well as her own spiritual development and faith in God. Even in the face of her own inevitable death and that of all her loved ones, Etty

Hillesum, 28 years old at the time, maintained a rare humanistic-spiritual outlook. "I really see no other solution than to turn inward and to root out all the rottenness there," she wrote. "I no longer believe that we can change anything in the world until we have first changed ourselves. And that seems to me the only lesson to be learned from this war. That we must look into ourselves and nowhere else."[17]

From Westerbork Transit Camp, Hillesum wrote: "The misery here is quite terrible; and yet, late at night when the day has slunk away into the depths behind me, I often walk with a spring in my step along the barbed wire. And then time and again, it soars straight from my heart—I can't help it, that's just the way it is, like some elementary force—the feeling that life is glorious and magnificent, and that one day we shall be building a whole new world."[18]

Etty lived a few blocks from Anne Frank. They both died in Nazi camps, Anne at Bergen-Belsen at 15, and Etty at Auschwitz, six weeks before her 30th birthday. Her mysticism has been likened to that of the French philosopher and mystic Simone Weil. Both women were born Jewish in Europe at the beginning of the 20th century, and both found, or were drawn toward, Christian ethics and spirituality.

As World War II and the holocaust grew more horrific, Etty wrote:

I see no other solution, I really see no other solution than to turn inward and to root out all the rottenness there. I no longer believe that we can change anything in the world until we have first changed ourselves. And that seems to me the only lesson to be learned from this war. That we must look into ourselves and nowhere else.[19]

Author and artist Fiona Alison Duncan writes regarding Etty that:

Etty Hillesum accepted early what she called "her destiny" —to die in the camps with her friends and family. Despite loved ones' urgings, she made no attempt to hide or flee. She even volunteered at Westerbork Transit Camp, where she worked for a month with the Social Welfare for People in Transit Department, shuttling neighbors into crowded trains destined for Poland and Germany. Later, she would be conscripted as an internee at that camp along with her parents and younger brother. On September 7, 1943, they were deported to Auschwitz, and all died within two months. [20]

Etty chose to become a mystic and a bodhisattva rather than an activist. She was passionately engaged in her inner life amid all the horror that was unfolding in the external world.

> "When you have an interior life," she wrote, "it certainly doesn't matter what side of the prison fence you're on... I've already died a thousand times in a thousand concentration camps. I know everything. There is no new information to trouble me. One way or another, I already know everything. And yet, I find this life beautiful and rich in meaning. At every moment."[21]

RACHEL CARSON

Probably the finest nature writer of the twentieth century, Rachel Carson warned of the dangers to all natural systems from the misuse of chemical pesticides such as DDT, questioned the scope and direction of modern science, and initiated the contemporary environmental movement. Because Carson asked the hard questions about whether and why humans had the right to control nature; to decide who lives or dies, and to poison or to destroy nonhuman life, attacks upon her would be inevitable. Her monumental work *Silent Spring* placed the work of agriculture and industry in the sinister context of profit-driven corporations and complicit government and educational institutions. They reacted with hostility to both author and book.[22]

Opponents of *Silent Spring* attacked Rachel Carson personally. They accused her of being radical, disloyal, unscientific, and hysterical. In 1962, at the height of the Cold War with the Soviet Union, criticism of the United States struck many as unpatriotic or sympathetic to communism. Former Secretary of Agriculture Ezra Taft Benson wrote privately to former President Dwight Eisenhower that Carson was "probably a communist."[23] Velsicol's threatening letter to Houghton Mifflin publishing company argued that if the public demanded elimination of pesticides, "our supply of food will be reduced to East-curtain parity [i.e., as inefficient as the Communist nations east of the 'Iron Curtain']."[24]

Carson had been diagnosed with cancer in 1960, which had metastasized due to her doctor's negligence. In 1963, when *Silent Spring* stirred President Kennedy's attention and he summoned a Congressional hearing to investigate and regulate the use of pesticides, Carson didn't hesitate to testify even as her body was giving out from the debilitating pain of the disease and the wearying radiation treatments. With her testimony as a pillar, JFK and his Science Advisory Committee invalidated her critics' arguments, heeded Carson's cautionary call to reason, and created the first federal policies designed to protect the planet.[25]

Carson endured the attacks—those of her cancer and those of her critics—with unwavering heroism. She saw the former with a biologist's calm acceptance of the cycle of life and had anticipated the latter all along. She was a spirited idealist, but she wasn't a naïve one—from the outset, she was acutely aware that her book was a clarion call for nothing less than a revolution and that it was her moral duty to be the revolutionary she felt called to be.[26]

Carson was deeply attached to her best friend, Dorothy Freeman, and with time, their relationship moved beyond platonic to romantic. Although Carson did not live within an authoritarian regime, the sexism and misogyny of her day wore heavily upon her, and love proved to be her sustaining and guiding force.

OUR ACTIVIST ANCESTORS

Countless role models of freedom and social justice from recent and distant history have left us a legacy of inspiration. On the one hand, the territory we tread in the twenty-first century is unique. Yet other ordinary men and women have suffered on behalf of their and our deepest humanity. We cannot know the extent to which we will be tested as climate catastrophe increases and systems collapse, but we can know that we are not alone. We can carry the role models of our choice in our hearts and draw on their wisdom and courage when we are tempted to despair.

The men and women named in this chapter are our activist ancestors. Although no longer with us, they have left us their stories and their actions. As Joanna Macy writes in *Coming Back to Life:*

Receive the creativity of your ancestors, making tools, weaving cloth, building homes.

The compassion of your ancestors, caring for the injured or praying with the dying: that, too, is for you.

Know their love of beauty, music of a flute coming from

the hills, hands carving jewelry, feet dancing to the rhythms of drums. Receive that celebration as their gift to you.

Know the intelligence of your ancestors as they track the movements of stars, learn the ways of the plants and animals, hold councils to choose the wisest action. Receive that intelligence as their gift.

Your ancestors have gifts from their suffering, too: courage, endurance, resilience, stubborn perseverance. Receive these as their gifts to you.[27]

FIERCE PRACTICES

These practices are more effective when we make time to journal and quietly reflect on them without interruption.

- Is there one person in this chapter in particular who inspires you as you navigate an authoritarian world?
- Who are some other people who inspire your sense of justice and courage? Many were not mentioned here: Martin Luther King, Jr., Harriett Tubman, Cesar Chavez, Rosa Parks, Greta Thunberg, Karen Silkwood, Dorothy Solle, Dorothy Day, Daniel Berrigan, Dalai Lama, Thich Nhat Hahn, and many more.
- What qualities in your role models do you most admire? What would help you develop those qualities within yourself?

CHAPTER 22
ARTIFICIAL INTELLIGENCE: IT'S PERSONAL

This is the existential contradiction of the second modernity that defines our conditions of existence: we want to exercise control over our own lives, but everywhere that control is thwarted. Individualization has sent each one of us on the prowl for the resources we need to ensure effective life, but at each turn we are forced to do battle with an economics and politics from whose vantage point we are but ciphers. We live in the knowledge that our lives have unique value, but we are treated as invisible. As the rewards of late-stage financial capitalism slip beyond our grasp, we are left to contemplate the future in a bewilderment that erupts into violence with increasing frequency. Our expectations of psychological self-determination are the grounds upon which our dreams unfold, so the losses we experience in the slow burn of rising inequality, exclusion, pervasive competition, and degrading stratification are not only economic. They slice us to the quick in dismay and bitterness because we know ourselves to be worthy of individual dignity and the right to a life on our own terms. —Shoshana Zuboff, The Age of Surveillance Capitalism: The Fight for a Human Future at the New Frontier of Power[1]

N o consideration of autocracy in the twenty-first century is adequate unless it includes a brief summary of Shoshona Zuboff's *The Age of Surveillance Capitalism*, a chilling exposé of the ominous uses of artificial intelligence to control human behavior in the name of corporate profits. In her words, "The tech giants use our data not only to predict our behavior but to change it. But we can resist this attack on democracy."[2]

As we go about comparing the global anti-democratic wave with the regimes of Nazi Germany or Bolshevik Russia, we are compelled to notice that those comparisons are limited by the technology Germany and Russia lacked which surveillance capitalism now accesses in the digital age. Today, we have avenues of exploiting and destroying democracy that Hitler and Stalin could have only dreamt of.

In a chilling *New York Times* article, Zuboff writes:

All of these delusions [about surveillance capitalism] rest on the most treacherous hallucination of them all: the belief that privacy is private. We have imagined that we can choose our degree of privacy with an individual calculation in which a bit of personal information is traded for valued services—a reasonable quid pro quo. For example, when Delta Air Lines piloted a biometric data system at the Atlanta airport, the company reported that of nearly 25,000 customers who traveled there each week, 98 percent opted into the process, noting that "the facial recognition option is saving an average of two seconds for each customer at boarding, or nine minutes when boarding a wide body aircraft.[3]

Similarly, Johann Hari, author of *Stolen Focus: Why You*

Can't Pay Attention and How to Think Deeply Again, argues that corporate capitalism, through social media, has impaired our ability to pay attention. So has multitasking. Summarizing her interview with Hari, *Washington Post* writer Angela Haupt concludes:

> Hari argues that, in fact, this constant switching between tasks is at the root of the attention crisis. There's been such an enormous increase in the volume of new information available every second that we've become transfixed by things that are "very fast and very temporary, like a Twitter feed." The more information we inhale, he says, the less we're able to focus on any one piece of it. Our brains aren't designed to absorb so much at a time
>
> Big-name websites and apps strive to distract because that's the key to profitability. When we're looking at our screens, these companies make money; when we're not, they don't. So they manipulate us to keep us there, scrolling and clicking. "Whenever you are tempted to put your phone down, the site keeps drip-feeding you the kind of material that it has learned, from your past behavior, keeps you scrolling," Hari writes.
>
> It doesn't have to be like this. There's an entirely different way our tech could work, he argues, and a world in which our healthy attention spans could exist in tandem with our phones and social media accounts. One easy example: Facebook could hold all notifications and deliver them to you once a day, rather than pinging you in real time and interrupting your focus. Or such sites could remove their infinite scroll, so when you reached the bottom of the screen, you had to think about whether you wanted to see more or not. These changes could be implemented overnight, but

without financial incentives, they're unlikely to come to fruition.[4]

But what we are consuming in the myriad distractions is not just "innocent information," but information that seduces us to buy products, pay for subscriptions, and engage with predatory capitalism in ways that damage our ability to pay attention and which provide gargantuan amounts of data about us as consumers.

Hari suggests that the opposite of our distracted state is the "flow state." Hari asserts that, "If you've ever experienced a flow state, you know what it is, though it can be difficult to put into words. Imagine an artist engrossed in the act of creation or a rock climber scaling an unfamiliar mountain." As Hari describes it: "This is when you are so absorbed in what you are doing that you lose all sense of yourself, and time seems to fall away, and you are flowing into the experience itself. It is the deepest form of focus and attention that we know of... To recover from the attention crisis, he argues, we need to replace our distractions with sources of flow."[5]

This could be the kind of "flow" I experience as I write this book or that anyone might experience in a creative project, in deep meditation, or in surrendering to deep intimacy with another person.

Science writer and computer scientist Erik Larson is one of the many reviewers of *The Age of Surveillance Capitalism*, Zuboff's book. He argues that at the moment, Big Tech companies that use artificial intelligence (AI), are interested in utilizing it only to increase their profits:

Zuboff's book is a masterpiece at framing the issue of AI— though her discussion of AI is derivative from her discussion of the Big Tech companies that employ it—as a form of control that tends to concentrate power in the hands of the owners of the systems—not the end users. What results is an Orwellian picture of modern life sans totalitarianism. Anti-democratic countries like China might celebrate expansion of surveillance in top-down fashion by Big Brother government, but Silicon Valley doesn't care about owning your soul or policing your thoughts. Your behavior online suffices. As Zuboff points out, Big Tech doesn't care what you say or do in the end (though, notoriously, it sometimes seemingly does, as with recent actions taken by Amazon, Facebook, and Twitter to limit certain types of political content). It simply needs to know more and more about you —where you go, what you eat, who you date, what you say in text messages, and of course what you search for online. That surplus is the key to their profits, and so is understandably guarded and defended in spite of mounting evidence that this newly discovered form of capitalism is virulent.[6]

Zuboff, on the other hand, argues that surveillance capitalism's use of AI is a much bigger deal:

They want to know the maximum they can extract from us in an exchange. They want to know how we will behave in order to know how to best intervene in our behavior. The best way to make your predictions desirable to customers is to ensure they come true: "to tune and herd and shape and push us in the direction that creates the highest probability of their business success." There's no way "to dress this up as anything but behavioral modification." In 2012 and 2013, Facebook conducted "massive-scale contagion experiments" to see if they could "affect real-world emotions and behavior, in ways that bypassed user awareness."[7]

Many nonfiction and science-fiction books have been written about AI, and perhaps Zuboff will delve deeper into the topic in future works, but what her research thus far has revealed is more than chilling. We know with certainty that many autocratic regimes have and will have access to technologically draconian implements of tyranny that are presently unimaginable. For example, *Scientific American* reports that *Mind Reading and Mind Control Technologies Are Coming*:

> The ability to detect electrical activity in the brain through the scalp, and to control it, will soon transform medicine and change society in profound ways. Patterns of electrical activity in the brain can reveal a person's cognition—normal and abnormal. New methods to stimulate specific brain circuits can treat neurological and mental illnesses and control behavior. In crossing this threshold of great promise, difficult ethical quandaries confront us.[8]

As Zuboff astutely summarizes:

> Surveillance capitalism really, as we said before, moves beyond the economic domain, to the societal domain, into our lives, threatening the very basis of a democratic social system. And that's where, to me, we now recognize that the time has come for us to name it, to understand it, to recognize that it's an economic logic that is not a necessary consequence of the digital or of the platform mechanism and that this is the time when we now, through understanding and through naming, we change our consciousness, we turn to our democratic institutions and reclaim democracy as a source of the law and the new regulatory institutions that are gonna intervene upon, interrupt, and outlaw these

mechanisms, so that the age of surveillance capitalism turns out to be a short age.[9]

As the United States, leader in AI technology, teeters on the edge of autocracy, a concerted effort to regulate surveillance capitalism and its potentially tyrannical uses of AI is unlikely. What is more likely is the use of AI to fortify autocracy and advance the agenda of a collapsing but ultimately coercive empire.

FIERCE PRACTICES

These practices are more effective when we make time to journal and quietly reflect on them without interruption.

- You may already be familiar with the information in this chapter, but what do you *feel* after reading it?
- How are you protecting yourself in real time from the invasiveness of technology?
- Assess your level of distraction by social media and by multitasking. What changes do you need to make?
- What activities allow you to drop deeply into "the flow"? What changes do you need to make?

CHAPTER 23
RESISTING TYRANNY

I'm not interested in retreat. I'm interested in resistance that also creates resilience and restoration, and I am not alone in that. All over the world—while working to hold nation-states and corporations to account for environmental pollution and destruction—groups are building systems of care, repair and resiliency that resist the despair and nihilism that can seep (or slosh or tsunami) into the work. —Frida Berrigan[1]

Since the election of Donald Trump to the Presidency of the United States in 2016, I have been captivated by the works of scholars whose expertise lies in the study of authoritarianism. The contemporary ones I most revere are: Timothy Snyder, Professor of History at Yale University, author of *On Tyranny*; Jason Stanley, Professor of Sociology at Yale, author of *How Fascism Works*; Ruth Ben-Ghiat, Professor of History and Italian Studies at New York University, author of *Strongmen: Mussolini to the Present*; and Barbara Walter, Professor of Political Science at the University of California, San

Diego, author of *How Civil Wars Start and How To Stop Them.*

As Trump was running for office, we heard frequent comments from media about Trump's fundamental illiteracy and what miniscule interest he ever displayed in reading a book. Rumor had it that the only book that ever held his interest was a book of speeches by Adolph Hitler which his former wife stated that he kept on the nightstand beside his bed.[2] He reportedly told his Chief of Staff in the White House, John Kelly, that "Hitler did a lot of good things."[3] Trump never declared that he was a fascist or sympathetic to fascism, but his words, actions, and policies throughout his Presidential term and in current time eerily embody the fascist mindset.

At this writing, we are receiving mindboggling revelations from the January 6 Select Committee in the United States Congress of Trump's lawless, tyrannical behavior during and at the end of his term in office. However, my focus in this chapter is not on Donald Trump per se, but the gargantuan fascist machinery that his Presidency set in motion and that threatens to engulf the democratic republic of the United States and mirrors authoritarian regimes such as Hungary, Brazil, the Philippines, Poland, the Democratic Republic of the Congo, Iran, Turkey, Saudi Arabia, China, and North Korea.

Even now as the authoritarian trajectory in the United States is becoming incontrovertibly blatant, many Americans remain in denial of its reality. The "it can't happen here" syndrome has infected those already suffering from the disease of American exceptionalism. The four scholars mentioned at the beginning of this chapter have painstakingly revealed that the United States is as vulnerable as any banana republic to being engulfed in tyrannical authoritarianism. At the moment, the political instrument that makes this possible and indeed probable is the Republican Party.

RESISTING TYRANNY

In his small but dynamic book, *On Tyranny*, Timothy Snyder offers twenty suggestions[4] for resisting tyranny in our societies which we must implement now and continue to deploy as authoritarianism seeks to prevail. I enthusiastically recommend becoming familiar with these twenty suggestions and engaging in them as much as humanly possible.

Journalist Masha Gessen, now living in the United States, has lived in autocracies most of her life. In her 2016 *New York Review of Books* article, written only a few days after Trump's Presidential election victory, "Autocracy: Rules for Survival," she offers several suggestions for survival and resistance:

Rule #1: Believe the autocrat. He means what he says. Whenever you find yourself thinking, or hear others claiming, that he is exaggerating, that is our innate tendency to reach for a rationalization. This will happen often: humans seem to have evolved to practice denial when confronted publicly with the unacceptable.

Rule #2: Do not be taken in by small signs of normality. Consider the financial markets this week [2016], which, having tanked overnight, rebounded following the Clinton and Obama speeches. Confronted with political volatility, the markets become suckers for calming rhetoric from authority figures. So do people. Panic can be neutralized by falsely reassuring words about how the world as we know it has not ended. It is a fact that the world did not end on November 8 nor at any previous time in history. Yet history has seen many catastrophes, and most of them unfolded over time.

Rule #3: Institutions will not save you. It took Putin a year to take over the Russian media and four years to dismantle its electoral system; the judiciary collapsed unnoticed. The capture of institutions in Turkey has been carried out even faster, by a man once celebrated as the democrat to lead Turkey into the EU. Poland has in less than a year undone half of a quarter century's accomplishments in building a constitutional democracy.

As Timothy Snyder suggests, do not rely on institutions to save you, but choose one that you would like to "save."

Rule #4: Be outraged. If you follow Rule #1 and believe what the autocrat-elect is saying, you will not be surprised. But in the face of the impulse to normalize, it is essential to maintain one's capacity for shock. This will lead people to call you unreasonable and hysterical, and to accuse you of overreacting. It is no fun to be the only hysterical person in the room. Prepare yourself.

Rule #5: Don't make compromises. Like Ted Cruz, who made the journey from calling Trump "utterly amoral" and a "pathological liar" to endorsing him in late September to praising his win as an "amazing victory for the American worker," Republican politicians have fallen into line. Conservative pundits who broke ranks during the campaign will return to the fold. Democrats in Congress will begin to make the case for cooperation, for the sake of getting anything done—or at least, they will say, minimizing the damage. Nongovernmental organizations, many of which are reeling at the moment, faced with a transition period in which there is no opening for their input, will grasp at chances to work with the new administration. This will be fruitless—damage cannot be minimized, much less reversed, when mobilization is the goal—but worse, it will be soul-destroying. In an autocracy, politics as the art of the possible is in fact utterly amoral. Those who argue for cooperation will make the case, much as President Obama did in his speech, that cooperation is essential for the future. They will be willfully ignoring the corrupting touch of autocracy, from which the future must be protected.

Rule #6: Remember the future. Nothing lasts forever. Donald Trump certainly will not, and Trumpism, to the extent that it is centered on Trump's persona, will not either. Failure to imagine the future may have lost the Democrats this election. They offered no vision of the future to counterbalance Trump's all-too-familiar white-populist vision of an imaginary past. They had also long ignored the strange and outdated institutions of American democracy that call out for reform—like the electoral college, which has now cost the Democratic Party two elections in which Republicans won with the minority of the popular vote. That should not be normal. But resistance—stubborn, uncompromising, outraged—should be.[5]

In his 2021 book, *How to Stop Fascism*, British journalist Paul Mason offers five actions we can take to confront authoritarianism:

1. *Study history and learn from it.* Fascism takes off when large numbers of people experience a kind of mass "religious" conversion to far right ideologies. We must oppose and expose racism in all its forms.
2. *We need a political alliance between the center and the left.* Fascism wants to kick off a global, racist, civil war. Support movements of freedom from oppression: Black Lives Matter, Me Too, LGBTQ rights, women's equality and reproductive rights.
3. *Recognize that Western society is in trouble.* We are afflicted with mass disorientation created by many factors, including a global pandemic. The

combination of mass disorientation with mass disillusionment with democracy is an ideal condition for burgeoning fascism. Who needs democracy when there is a man or authoritarian figure who can solve all of society's problems?

4. *Be a proud, active anti-fascist.* We must carry an ethos of anti-fascism in our daily lives. Fascism in the 1930s was defeated by people who made a moral commitment to defeat it.

5. *We need new anti-fascist laws and regulations* such as: Banning uniformed parades which is the militarization of public space; regulating social media when it posts false information; severely penalizing people who make death threats.

While we dare not pretend that we can be wide-eyed or simple-minded about the rising tide of authoritarianism, we must remember that some successful political movements have appealed to our humanity more than law and order or repression and hatred. Ruth Ben-Ghiat cites one example in an interview with journalist Joanne Lipman:

The most recent [movement]—which I'm very interested in —happened in Turkey with the race for the campaign for mayor of Istanbul. Ekrem İmamoğlu ran for mayor as an opposition candidate. He had a platform he called "Radical Love." Instead of preaching vertical obedience to authority and hatred, he walked around the streets of Istanbul and he embraced people. He went to where they were, face to face, and he refused to engage in polarizing and negative campaigning. And this has enormous appeal. So he won the race for mayor of Istanbul causing the Erdoğan government to use technicalities to annul the results. Because that's what autocrats do.

They made them have a rematch. And İmamoğlu persisted in his positive campaigning and he got, the second time around, even more votes. So, he's now the mayor of Istanbul and he's published articles—including in the *Washington Post*—about how he feels this approach can beat polarization and give hope to people. Basically, he gave a message of optimism, caring, and hope.

I say bleak things if I need to, but I believe that there is a hunger in the human heart for a more just kind of government.[6]

I am captivated by Ben-Ghiat's last sentence—a "hunger in the human heart for a more just kind of government." In these moments of madness and rampant authoritarianism in our world, it is difficult to notice that hunger, yet I would not have written this book if I did not believe it exists. It is palpable in the words of Snyder, Stanley, Ben-Ghiat, Walter, and Paul Mason. In the coming years, we may be unable to avoid bearing witness to the rages of fascism which may even touch our own lives very personally. In order to persevere, we will need to understand and open to the grace that suffering offers us, and no topic is more appropriate for ending this book.

FIERCE PRACTICES

These practices are more effective when we make time to journal and quietly reflect on them without interruption.

If we are willing to fiercely practice shadow healing, we are compelled to explore our own "inner autocrat." The human psyche contains some autocratic impulses, and we need to begin with the ones we are aware of within ourselves if we are to confront external autocrats. A common one is a "need" to control our lives and the lives of others. Our ability to control is much more limited than we would like to believe. It may be helpful to make a list of all of the things we *cannot* control.

We all have an inner "strongman" (regardless of our gender) who convinces us that we cannot afford to be vulnerable. Take time to journal about your fears of being vulnerable. Have you ever experienced that being vulnerable was empowering for yourself or someone else?

What are actions that you are taking or can take to confront autocracy and tyranny in your community and your country? Remembering Timothy Snyder's suggestion to befriend an institution, is there an institution that you want to befriend and help fortify?

CHAPTER 24

HUMANITY'S RITE OF PASSAGE

Initiation means a rite of passage from one stage of life to another. The absence of formal initiation in the West is why young people create their own informal initiations, such as engaging in reckless and dangerous behavior. Maybe drug addicts and alcoholics are trying to break into a different state of reality, as happens in a true initiation. The problem is their initiations never end.

In a functioning society initiation raises awareness of life's purpose and is not just oriented toward getting a job and making a living. We each need to have a personal mission that contributes to the well-being of the world. Finding one's purpose is the primary goal of initiation. It also teaches responsibility toward community, village, and culture. The indigenous formula says that we all come into this world with a gift that we must give to the world. We must undergo initiation to discover what our gift is and how to share it. —Malidoma Somé[1]

A rite of passage is a ceremony that marks the passage from one developmental, social, or religious status to another. What is remarkable about the rite of passage is its nearly universal presence in vastly different ancient cultures globally and throughout history. In numerous ancient cultures, and still in some cultures around the world today, young people are prepared from birth to participate in a rite of passage near the age of puberty which marks their transition from childhood to adulthood. This usually involves a challenge which may be physical, intellectual, emotional, and spiritual and will require rigorous personal growth. To honor the initiate's personal transformation, the ceremony is often followed by a celebration and welcoming from the community.

It is important to understand that rite of passage ceremonies vary significantly from culture to culture. There is no "one" or "correct" ceremony, but most traditional cultures of the past have created their own according to their experiences of what is useful to their communities. Some of those ceremonies or remnants of them are still practiced in certain indigenous communities today.

The rite of passage or initiation ritual involves three fundamental elements:

- A vision of possibility: From birth and through childhood, a young person is prepared for his or her rite of passage. A key aspect of the preparation is understanding why they need the rite, how they will rise to the challenge, and what it can help them accomplish in life and in the community.
- An ordeal or series of ordeals which are a set of grueling physical and emotional challenges
- A homecoming and celebration which

acknowledges and supports the young person's
new role in the community.

While many present-day cultures may no longer have
formal rites of passage, historically, cultures throughout the
world believed that they were necessary. The initiation usually
involved some type of challenge that not only required
endurance and physical and emotional rigor, but also
compelled the young person to reach down inside themselves
to discover a deeper identity. In other words, the challenge
revealed to them that they are more than a mind or an ego and
that they are also a spiritual, transcendent being.

Carl Jung believed that although we do not have formal
initiations in the modern world, we nevertheless have initiatory experiences in all aspects of our lives. Jung taught that the
rite of passage is an archetype or universal theme that resides
within the human psyche that we encounter regularly, even if
the encounter is not recognized as a formal initiation.

For example, experiencing a divorce, losing a job, receiving
a diagnosis of terminal illness, a car accident, the death of a
loved one—all have some emotional ordeal baked in. The
ordeal may be major or minor from the standpoint of the
person experiencing it, but it is part of the initiatory process.
Jung saw these informal initiations as symbolic of the literal
process, but no less significant. He argued that in the absence
of literal initiations, the archetype of initiation within the
human psyche utilizes everyday adversity to assist in our
evolution.

At the core of the ancient indigenous community's world
view was a deep and intimate connection with nature. Nature
was sacred to them, and so was the spirit of every living being.
The community believed that if the young person did not have
an initiatory, nature-based experience, they would have diffi-

culty connecting with the sacred within themselves and in the world. Without experiencing that they were a sacred being, they would never really become a mature human being, and as a result, they would actually become toxic to the community. For this reason, the community was willing to risk the possibility that the young person might not physically survive the ordeal. Usually, they did survive, but sometimes they did not.

PREPARATION FROM BIRTH

An ancient, indigenous child came to the formal initiation ritual after lifelong preparation for it. Family and elders taught children about the importance of initiation and gave them a vision of possibility. In other words, they *INspired* the child to *ASpire* to the rite of passage by teaching them that because of what they experience by going through it, they will be able to live more meaningful lives and take their rightful place of leadership in the community.

Unlike our ancient, indigenous ancestors, we have not been prepared for either literal or symbolic initiations. In fact, Western culture's narcissistic entitlement is symptomatic of our grievous loss of rites of passage. In traditional cultures that provided initiatory rituals, adversity was viewed as a tragic aspect of life inherent in the human condition, not an anomaly from which we should be spared because the ego feels it should be exempt.

THE INITIATION OF A SPECIES

Understanding the archetype of initiation and its imperative in the human psyche has enabled me to reframe our planetary predicament as an invitation to become a new species of human that transcends the outcome of the ordeal. That is to say that evolution, not survival or superiority, is the endgame. In other words, humanity is currently in the throes of a mystical, psycho-spiritual initiation.

Our planetary rite of passage holds many possibilities. It has the potential to make us more resilient as individuals, and it also has the potential to uniquely inform us about how to live more compassionately and more skillfully in order to deeply adapt and help heal the planet. It reveals the fullness of our humanity and the possibilities for creating healthier ecosystems, healthier communities, and wiser and more compassionate individuals.

The rite of passage is not just for the initiate; it benefits the entire community. The newly initiated young person was taught that as she or he moved into the homecoming phase of the process, it would be important to consider how they might apply their own personal gifts, talents, or skills in the larger community. During the initiation, elders discussed this with initiates so that the young person understood that the ordeal equipped them to serve, and that their individual gifts could guide them in doing so.

THE CONVERGENCE OF THE LITERAL AND SYMBOLIC

Practically speaking, as we navigate the regular symbolic initiations in our personal lives in the twenty-first century, our experience is similar to the young person who came through a formal rite of passage. Processing our experience of a symbolic initiation is crucial. For example, with what attitude did we meet the initiation? What emotions did we encounter? What adversities did we face physically, financially, logistically? Who were our allies? Or did we find ourselves alone and without allies? What symbolic or literal deaths did we experience? What did we discover about ourselves that we did not know before the initiation? Did the experience deepen our compassion for ourselves and for others? Did the experience infuse us with gratitude for what is good and beautiful in our lives? What counsel would we offer others who are experiencing a symbolic rite of passage?

These same questions can be asked regarding our planetary predicament in this moment and the collective initiation our species is undergoing.

When we understand the rite of passage motif, it is virtually impossible to deny that our planet is experiencing a collective initiation. Our species is embroiled in the cataclysm of a dying planet, protracted war, possibly recurring global pandemics, massive economic inequality, rampant racism, the epidemic spread of political authoritarianism, and unprecedented cultural and political division at a moment when unity is required to address any of these issues.

When we understand that we are engaged in a planetary rite of passage, our view widens, and our perspective is enlarged. Our view from, as they say, 35,000 feet informs our actions and makes them more strategic. If this is an initiation, then there are no "solutions"; there are only responses. That does not mean that we do nothing or simply give up and abdicate our responsibility. We continue to act, but we act as well-informed initiates, passing through an ordeal in which we daily surrender the ego to the Self and allow our gifts to be unleashed on behalf of the Self and the Earth community.

If we view our predicament as an initiation, we can accept climate meltdown and the collapse of systems more fully. Earlier, I noted Francis Weller's perspective of becoming an "apprentice of sorrow." Is it not utterly urgent that we become apprentices of our predicament? Only by doing so can we experience the benefits of becoming its students.

Let me be clear: I am not implying that the transformation

of *consciousness* that comes as a result of planetary or personal initiation is going to spare us from experiencing the *consequences* of our estrangement from and disrespect of nature. Furthermore, I do not wholeheartedly resonate with the notion that we are "spiritual beings having a human experience." It is equally true that we are human beings having spiritual experiences that our souls crave, but that does not make us any less human.

Richard Tarnas, in his book, *Is the Modern Psyche Undergoing a Rite of Passage?* asks:

"Are we going to make it?" He states:

> We cannot be completely sure that we will. No authentic initiatory process begins in the certainty of its outcome. It is not at all certain that we will successfully pass through this eye of the needle, this planetary ego death. For the foreseeable future, we seem to be living in an era of high drama. We seem to be engaged now in a kind of race...between initiation and catastrophe.[2]

From my perspective, "Are we going to make it?" is the wrong question. As you would expect, I must return to the only two questions that matter: *Who do I want to be, and what did I come here to do?*

FIERCE PRACTICES

These practices are more effective when we make time to journal and quietly reflect on them without interruption.

- What symbolic initiations have you experienced?
- Choose one of those and write about how you

responded immediately after and beyond. What experiences and insights resulted from the ordeal?

- In that ordeal or perhaps another one, did you sense any tempering of the ego or any expansion of the Self?
- In the context of our current planetary rite of passage, what internal resources have you experienced that have humbled the ego but expanded the Self?
- What personal lessons are you being taught in the throes of humanity's collective rite of passage?
- What benefits are you experiencing from accepting our predicament?

CHAPTER 25

GRACE: A BRIEF COMMUNION WITH THE FRAGILITY OF LIFE

But when you look at it from the spiritual point of view, you see that suffering is grace, a gift given in order to awaken you. Once you want to awaken, then the meaning of suffering changes. You don't court it, but when it comes down the pike, you work with it, because you see that it's a valuable vehicle. —Ram Dass[1]

God comes to you disguised as your life. —Paula D'Arcy[2]

Grace comes from knowing that to be alive and conscious in this world is a rare gift. If we are open to it, we can see that there is grace all around us, with or without God. —Katherine Ozment, *Grace Without God: The Search for Meaning, Purpose and Belonging in a Secular Age*[3]

The concept of grace is alive in many spiritual traditions. For Christians, grace means that even though we do not deserve forgiveness when we have done something wrong, God is ready and willing to forgive us. Buddhist author Mark Nepo writes that "Grace comes to the heart when it realizes what it is made of and what it has risen from. In that moment, grace comforts us, that no matter the joy or pain along the way, we are already a part of where we are going. Enlightenment for a heart on Earth is the moment we accept that it is the loving that makes waves of us all, again and again." But what does Nepo mean by "makes waves of us"? He clarifies:

> Profoundly, grace comes to the wave when it realizes what it is made of. Since it has risen from the very same water into which it will crash, its fear of ending is somehow lessened. For it is already a part of where it is going. Can it be that you and I, like simple waves, experience such an enlightenment the instant we realize that we are all made of the same water?[4]

Eastern spiritual teacher Ram Dass asserted that all suffering is imbued with grace because it is intended to awaken us to who we truly are—that we are sacred beings who constantly crash into the ocean of interconnectedness with all that is. Suffering is not a punishment, but rather a signpost that there is much more to learn about our authentic identity.

In the reformed tradition of Won Buddhism, grace isn't something that we receive from God or some higher power. Grace comes from recognizing and appreciating the indispensable relationships in our lives... not only are we interrelated, but our individual existence is also indebted to one another. This realization of interconnection and indebtedness allows us to be more understanding, responsible, and selfless.[5]

In other words, everything—even our suffering—is on some level a gift. We need not like it or feel happy about it, and it is never "fair," but perhaps we suffer less if we can hold the possibility that it is a gift to us—an opportunity to experience Interbeing.

Buddhist teacher Pema Chodron famously emphasizes in her teachings the human need to open the heart in order to heal and to demonstrate compassion to others. "To the degree that you didn't understand in the past how to stop protecting your soft spot," she says, "how to stop armoring your heart, you're given this gift of teachings in the form of your life, to give you everything you need to open further."[6]

THE GRACE AND THE ACCOUNTABILITY OF ENDINGS

In another missive by Mark Nepo, he speaks of gratitude as a doorway to grace:

> We enter the sanctity of our being in the simplest moments —while playing with animals and watching birds fly or standing in the dark awash with the shimmer of the moon, or watching a loved one wake into their truth. These uncluttered openings are the bare bones of grace. We could name grace *the unnamable presence that lives under all we do or aspire to.* (Nepo's emphasis)
>
> When stopped at the bedroom door while stepping into the day, when the quiet warmth of our nest makes me realize how precious and irreplaceable the simplest things are, then what I'm given is more than enough and I am grateful. In this way, *grace appears as a brief communion with the fragility of life.* It changes how we move through the thousand tasks that lie before us.[7]

As I continue to witness the fast track earthlings have chosen on the way to potential extinction, I am once again compelled to point to "the unnamable presence that lives under all we do or aspire to do," which is precisely why I have written this book.

In *Hospicing Modernity*, Vanessa Machado de Oliveira Andreotti writes that:

> Before anything different can happen, before people can sense, hear, relate, and imagine differently, there must be a clearing, a decluttering, an initiation into the unknowable; and a letting go of the desires for certainty, authority, hierarchy, and of insatiable consumption as a mode of relating to everything. We will need a genuine severance that will shatter all projections, anticipations, hopes, and expectations in order to find something we lost about ourselves, about time/space, about the depth of the shit we are in, about the medicines/poisons we carry. This is about pain, about death, about finding a compass, an antidote to separability. This is about being ready to go—to befriend death—before we are ready to return home and to live as grownups.[8]

Machado warns us that hospicing modernity "involves *intellectual accountability* and *existential surrender*... Intellectual accountability is about facing the truth behind our denials and projections; sitting with our complicity in harm; shedding arrogance and accepting accountability without seeking recognition, redemption, innocence, or purity. Existential surrender is about interrupting addictions and business as usual, confronting fragilities, learning to compost personal and collective shit, and relinquishing colonial entitlements.[9]

None of this is primarily a project or product of intellect. Fundamentally, it is about a diligent commitment to daily psycho-spiritual work. From my perspective, no one has elucidated this with more laser clarity than Zach Stein:

For those identifying as spiritual or religious: yes, this is why you have been sitting on the mat, praying, and "working on your Self." But the liminal may require you to re-examine your ideas concerning reality, especially the notion that you create your own...Living between worlds means dealing (again) with reality itself, which is not some featureless totality of oneness, but a complex non-dual whole in which every choice counts and has causal impact. This is one of the reasons our situation today demands actual self-transformation: you can't bullshit yourself anymore. Now you will get to see if you actually know how to meditate and act in a selfless way; not when you want to, when you have to.

Finding meaning in tragedy is a perennial human task, as is the task of remaking of the self. We must learn to do both while creating a new world. Grief is warranted. Fear is warranted. Pain is inevitable. But in so far as the future matters, learning must become our primary process. Adaptation, evolution, transformation, rebirth, metamorphosis, metanoia, and change—we are in for all of it, and in short order. These are experiences one might seek out for adventure and growth during saner times; today they are thrust upon us all. Returning to reality is the nature of the liminal, and reality is relationship, not isolation.[10]

At the conclusion of Adam McKay's brilliant 2022 movie *Don't Look Up*, a comet is about to decimate the Earth after numerous warnings from the scientists who discovered it. Although the majority of humans on Earth dismiss the inevitability of destruction, the scientists, with their families and friends, gather around a dinner table. At this time nothing can be done to stop the cataclysm. In a tender moment, as they sit together ready to enjoy their meal, they are well aware that their death is imminent, and every second feels more precious than the previous one. They hold hands, and one person offers a prayer. The dishes, the table, and the entire house begins rattling and convulsing. Cameras fade as life on Earth ceases, and we are left to contemplate the final moments of those specific people around that particular table with the searing awareness that in the end, the most cherished hours are those we share with each other in heartful intimacy and communion.

Our work is not to be heroes and s/heroes in the face of climate chaos, unbridled authoritarianism, and the collapse of systems. Many of us will not physically survive the bottleneck through which humanity is passing, especially as the bottleneck narrows. Even as I abhor "How long do we have?" questions and refuse to engage with them, I am well aware that a partially or totally "uninhabitable Earth" is closer than we can imagine. At the same time, outrageously fierce grace is waiting for our acceptance of humanity's predicament and a willing immersion into the inner and outer work that letting go of resistance to civilization's demise requires. Yes, grace is a "brief communion with the fragility of life" and in the same moment, an inexorable force that empowers us to live fiercely and undaunted—not in the silos of hyper-individualism or narcissistic entitlement, but within the generous, compassionate unknowns within Indra's net. It is only there that grace can find and hold us in this holy *catastrophe*.

FIERCE PRACTICES

These practices are more effective when we make time to journal and quietly reflect on them without interruption.

- What is your most memorable experience of "a brief communion with the fragility of life"?

- What is your experience of "the unnamable presence that lives under all we do or aspire to do"?
- Take time to reflect on the statement: "Grace comes from recognizing and appreciating the indispensable relationships in our lives... not only are we interrelated, but our individual existence is also indebted to one another. This realization of interconnection and indebtedness allows us to be more understanding, responsible, and selfless."
- What are some of the indispensable relationships in your life?

AFTERWORD

As I was concluding the final pages of this book, Russia invaded Ukraine on February 24, 2022. United States intelligence had detected the likelihood of the invasion some months prior and began warning Ukraine and the world. Understandably, most Ukrainians were in denial of the intelligence and therefore found themselves woefully unprepared for the devastation that ensued.

Since the invasion, the carnage in Ukraine has been horrific, with Russian President Putin obviously hell-bent on obliterating Ukraine's military and installing a puppet regime to rule the country—which he claims is not a real country. At this writing, Putin appears bitter, angry, and thoroughly uninterested in negotiating an end to the war. With thousands of Russian soldiers killed or injured and the invasion not producing the swift and speedy result that Putin wanted, he appears cornered—and as we know, a cornered, angry individual, determined to restore a lost empire as his final legacy to his country, is exceedingly dangerous.

Thus, this book ends not just with a deep analysis of climate chaos and a global pandemic, two of the most formidable events in modern history, but now with the real possibility of a world war in which the use of nuclear weapons is an even more frightening prospect. In other words, our global predicament just became even more extreme.

Who among us is not horrified by the severity of our predicament in this moment? Our descent as a species into the territory of a planetary rite of passage seems undeniable.

At the same time that our species' prognosis has become more appalling, the urgency of employing the tools offered above has never been more acute. At the same time that we beg to shy away, something more profound within us wants to take us to the depths of our humanness and the transformation of consciousness that *cata-strophe* offers.

Carl Jung once wrote:

No one should deny the danger of the descent, but it can be risked. No one need to risk it, but it is certain that someone will. And let those who go down the sunset way do so with open eyes, for it is a sacrifice which daunts even the gods. Yet every descent is followed by an ascent; the vanishing shapes are shaped anew, and a truth is valid in the end only if it suffers change and bears new witness in new images, in new tongues, like a new wine that is put into new bottles. [1]

As Anne Frank wrote her diaries in fearful seclusion, not knowing when she might be discovered; as Nelson Mandela languished in prison not knowing when he might be killed; as Rachel Carson struggled with the pain and fatigue of breast cancer in a world that did not value her brilliant, luminous insights into our extraordinary planet, we hold the tension of opposites from moment to moment, not knowing our future. This demise *is* sacred because while we may or may not feel undaunted in the descent, it is "a sacrifice which daunts even the gods" and makes a seemingly impossible ascent possible.

NOTES

FOREWORD

1. Ella Cara Deloria, *Waterlily*, University of Nebraska Press, 1988.
2. Ibid.

INTRODUCTION

1. "Post-Doom Benefits of Accepting Collapse," Karen Perry and Michael Dowd, February 20, 2022, https://www.youtube.com/watch?v=mhKbOtZM01c
2. "Climate Change Enters the Therapy Room," Ellen Barry, *New York Times*, February 6, 2022, https://www.nytimes.com/2022/02/06/health/climate-anxiety-therapy.html
3. A Conversation with Michael Dowd, "Living Well Now," YouTube, February, 2022, https://www.youtube.com/watch?v=S_CYxetOc1o&t=5s
4. "Our Foundational Commitment," Richard Rohr, Center for Action and Contemplation website, January, 2020, https://cac.org/themes/contemplation-and-action-part-one/

PART I

1. David Wallace-Wells, *The Uninhabitable Earth: Life after Warming*, Tim Duggan Books, 2019, p. 11.
2. Vanessa Machado de Oliveira. *Hospicing Modernity* (p. ix). North Atlantic Books. Kindle Edition.

1. EMOTIONS AS ALLIES, NOT ENEMIES

1. "Naomi Klein: Now let's fight back against the politics of fear," Naomi Klein, *Guardian*, June 10, 2017, https://www.theguardian.com/books/2017/jun/10/naomi-klein-now-fight-back-against-politics-fear-shock-doctrine-trump
2. Richard Leider, *The Power of Purpose: Find Meaning, Live Longer, Better*, Berrett-Koehler Publishers, p. 5.

3. Viktor Frankl, *Man's Search for Meaning : An Introduction to Logotherapy*, Boston: Beacon Press, 1962, p. 87.

4. "Unraveling Anxiety," Judy Lief, Lion's Roar, February 4, 2022, https://www.lionsroar.com/unraveling-anxiety/

2. THE FOLLY OF FEARLESSNESS

1. Pema Chodron, *When Things Fall Apart: Heart Advice for Difficult Times*, Shambala, 2002, p. 34.

2. "A Time of Conscious Descent," *Living Myth Podcast* #166, Michael Meade, https://www.mosaicvoices.org/episode-166-a-time-of-conscious-descent

3. Paul Levy, *The Quantum Revelation: A Radical Synthesis of Science and Spirituality*, Select Books, New York, 2018, p. 41.

3. BACKSTROKING IN THE RAGING RIVERS OF GRIEF

1. Francis Weller, *The Wild Edge of Sorrow*, North Atlantic, 2015, p. xviii.

2. Stephen Jenkinson, *Die Wise: A Manifesto for Soul and Sanity*, North Atlantic, 2015, p. 35.

3. Jeff Brown, *Grounded Spirituality*, Enrealment Press, 2019, p. 209.

4. Francis Weller, www.francisweller.net

5. David Kessler, https://www.davidkesslertraining.com/

6. Good Grief Network, https://www.goodgriefnetwork.org/

7. "An Apprenticeship with Sorrow," Francis Weller, https://www.francisweller.net/an-apprenticeship-with-sorrow.html

8. Francis Weller in conversation with Charles Eisenstein. *"Of Grief and Reverence" Podcast*, https://charleseisenstein.org/podcasts/new-and-ancient-story-podcast/episode-04-grief-and-reverence/

9. *American Psychological Association*, "Is Climate Grief Something New?" https://www.apa.org/members/content/climate-grief

10. "When Climate Change Enters the Therapy Room," *New York Times*, February 6, 2022, https://www.nytimes.com/2022/02/06/health/climate-anxiety-therapy.html

11. Francis Weller, *The Wild Edge of Sorrow*, North Atlantic, 2015, p. 220.

4. TITRATING WOKENESS

1. "How 'Woke' Became the Word of Our Era," Kenya Hunt, *Guardian*, November 21, 2021, https://www.theguardian.com/books/2020/nov/21/how-woke-became-the-word-of-our-era

NOTES

2. "What Does It Mean to be Woke?" Raven Cras, September, 2015, https://blavity.com/what-does-it-mean-to-be-woke?category1=opinion
3. https://www.britannica.com/science/titration

5. THEY DON'T SEE WHAT I SEE

1. ON WELTSCHMERZ AND WELTANSCHAUUNGEN, Jonathan Rowson, https://www.whatisemerging.com/opinions/on-weltschmerz-and-weltanschauungen
2. Richard Rohr, *Falling Upward: A Spirituality for the Two Halves of Life*, Josey-Bass, 2011, p. 102.
3. "Defense Mechanism," *Wikipedia*, https://en.wikipedia.org/wiki/Defence_mechanism#:~:text=In%20the%20first%20definitive%20book,introjection%2C%20turning%20against%20one's%20own
4. Stephen Jenkinson, *Die Wise*, p. 15.
5. "What If We Are All We've Got?" Zhiwa Woodbury, December 6, 2021, https://thubtenzhiwa.medium.com/what-if-we-are-all-weve-got-f2af6b3bdaed

6. DEEP ADAPTATION

1. *Deep Adaptation Forum*, Professions Network, https://deepadaptation.ning.com/about-us
2. *Deep Adaptation Forum*, https://www.deepadaptation.info/about/
3. "Deep Adaptation," *Wikipedia*, https://en.wikipedia.org/wiki/Deep_Adaptation
4. *Ibid.*

7. UNALTERABLE UNCERTAINTY

1. Jamie Holmes, *Nonsense: The Power of Not Knowing*, Crown, 2015, p. 84, quoted in "In Praise of Intellectual Uncertainty," by Matthew Hutson, *Washington Post*, November 13, 2015, https://www.washingtonpost.com/opinions/in-praise-of-intellectual-uncertainty/2015/11/11/77f71994-7103-11e5-8248-98e0f5a2e830_story.html
2. "The Fundamental Ambiguity of Being Human, Pema Chodron, *Tricycle Magazine*, Fall, 2021, https://tricycle.org/magazine/fundamental-ambiguity-being-human/
3. "Asian Economic Trends and Their Security Implications," by Charles Wolf Jr., Anil Bamezai, K. C. Yeh, and Benjamin Zycher. Chapter One, p. 1, published by Rand, Santa Monica, California. (Questia) 2000.
4. Jamie Holmes, *Nonsense: The Power of Not Knowing*.

5. Jane Hirshfield, *Hiddenness, Uncertainty, Surprise: Three Generative Energies of Poetry*, Bloodaxe Books, March, 2008, p. 72.
6. Meg Wheatley, *New Republic of the Heart Podcast*, May, 2020, https://newrepublicoftheheart.org/podcast/028-meg-wheatley-warriors-wanted-its-time-to-defend-the-human-spirit/
7. Margaret Wheatley, *Perseverance*, Berrett-Koehler Publishers, 2010, p. 15.

8. WHAT MATTERS MOST?

1. Viktor Frankl, *Man's Search for Meaning*, Beacon Press, 2006, p. 52.
2. "Covid 19: A War Broke Out In Heaven," Zachary Stein, March 26, 2020, https://www.whatisemerging.com/opinions/covid-19-a-war-broke-out-in-heaven
3. Jeremy Lent, *The Patterning Instinct*, Prometheus, 2017, p.48.
4. *Ibid.*, p. 212.
5. *Ibid.*, p. 252-252.
6. Jacqui Lewis, *Fierce Love: Fierce Love: A Bold Path to Ferocious Courage and Rule-Breaking Kindness That Can Heal the World* , New York: Harmony Books, 2021, pp. 11–12.
7. *Ibid.*, p. 302.
8. *Ibid.*, p. 316.
9. *Ibid.*, p. 317.
10. *Ibid.*, p. 321.
11. Thich Nhat Hahn, *Call Me By My True Names*, Parallax Press, 1999, p.73

9. RECOVERING FROM ADDICTION TO HOPE

1. "From Hope to Hopelessness," *Margaret Wheatley Website*, 2002, https://www.margaretwheatley.com/articles/fromhopetohopelessness.html
2. *Ibid.*
3. *Ibid.*
4. Stephen Jenkinson, *Come of Age: The Case for Elderhood in a Time of Trouble*, North Atlantic, 2018, p. 386.
5. *Ibid.* pp387-388.
6. "Willing To Be Disturbed," Meg Wheatley, *Turning to One Another: Simple Conversations to Restore Hope to the Future*, Berrett-Koehler Publications, 2002.
7. "The Place Beyond Fear and Hope," https://www.margaretwheatley.com/articles/BeyondHopeandFear.pdf

10. COMPASSION IS NOT FOR SISSIES

1. Pema Chodron, *The Places That Scare You*, Pema Chodron, 2002, p. 28.
2. Carl Jung, *Collected Works 11*, "Psychology and Religion," 1938, p.131.
3. Pema Chodron, *Comfortable with Uncertainty: 108 Teachings on Cultivating Fearlessness and Compassion*, Shambhala Publications, 2003, p.73,
4. "Love Crosses Boundaries," *Center for Action and Contemplation*, Daily Meditations, January 7, 2022, https://cac.org/love-crosses-boundaries-2022-01-07/
5. Connie Zweig, *The Inner Work of Age*, Park St. Press, 2021, pp. 60-61.
6. Paul Levy, *Wétiko: Healing the Mind-Virus That Plagues Our World*, Simon & Schuster, 2021, p. 9.
7. *Ibid.*, p. 12, 15.
8. *Ibid.*, p. 137.
9. *Ibid.*, p.226.
10. *Ibid.*, p. 239.

11. TRANSFORMING THE CONCEPT OF "CARE" AND "COMMUNITY"

1. Frank Schaeffer, *Fall in Love, Have Children, Stay Put, Save the Planet, Be Happy*, Health Communications, Boca Raton, 2021, p. 183.
2. Dalai Lama XIV, The Dalai Lama: A Policy of Kindness: An Anthology of Writings By and About the Dalai Lama
3. Frank Schaeffer, *op. cit.*, p. 54.
4. *Ibid.*, p. 216.
5. *Ibid.*, p. 313.
6. "Raising My Child in a Doomed World," Roy Scranton, *New York Times*, July 16, 2018, https://www.nytimes.com/2018/07/16/opinion/climate-change-parenting.html
7. *Ibid.*

12. I LOVE YOU, SON, BUT I LOVE FOSSIL FUELS MORE

1. Greta Thunberg, Twitter, https://twitter.com/AOC/status/1076890299773976582
2. "How to talk to children about climate change," Emma Patee, *Wired Magazine*, October 31, 2021, https://www.wired.com/story/how-to-talk-to-children-about-climate-change/
3. *Extinction Rebellion Youth*: https://xryouthus.org/

4. "How to Talk to Children About Climate Change," Emma Patee, *Wired Magazine*, October 31, 2021, https://www.wired.com/story/how-to-talk-to-children-about-climate-change/

13. COMING OF AGE AT THE END OF AN AGE

1. Zweig, *The Inner Work of Age*, p. 51.
2. Stephen Jenkinson, *Come of Age: The Case for Elderhood in a Time of Trouble*, North Atlantic, 2018, p. 22.
3. *Ibid.*, p. 388.
4. *Ibid.*, p. 55.

14. EARTH CARE, SELF-CARE: SACRED NATURE

1. Mundaka Upanishads, 3:1, Wisdom Library, Mundaka Upanishad, https://www.wisdomlib.org/hinduism/book/mundaka-upanishad-shankara-bhashya/d/doc145122.html
2. *Earth Charter Podcasts*, Gus Speth, https://earthcharter.org/podcasts/gus-speth/
3. Thomas Berry, *The Sacred Universe: Earth, Spirituality, and Religion in the Twenty-First Century*, Columbia University Press, 2009, p. 70.
4. Victoria Loorz, *Church of the Wild: How Nature Invites Us into the Sacred* (Minneapolis, MN: Broadleaf Books, 2021), 19–20, 21.
5. Newell, J. Philip. *Sacred Earth, Sacred Soul*, HarperCollins, 2021, p.6.
6. *Earth and Soul Website*, https://www.earthandsoul.org/
7. *Sacred Earth, Sacred Soul*, p. 40.
8. Thomas Berry, *The Sacred Universe*, p. 119.
9. Ibid., p. 74
10. *Ibid.*, p. 74
11. "Including the Earth in Our Prayers," Llewellyn Vaughn-Lee, Kosmos Journal, Fall, 2019, https://www.kosmosjournal.org/kj_article/spiritual-practice-as-a-catalyst-for-change/
12. "The Insight of Interbeing," Thich Nhat Hahn, Garrison Institute, https://www.garrisoninstitute.org/blog/insight-of-interbeing/
13. *Sacred Earth, Sacred Soul*, p. 160.
14. *Ibid.*, p. 190.

15. THE LIMITS OF THE RATIONAL MIND AND THE HUMAN EGO

1. Cynthia Bourgeault, *The Wisdom Way of Knowing: Reclaiming an Ancient Tradition to Awaken the Heart*, Josey-Bass Publishing, 2003, P.4.
2. Paul Levy, *The Quantum Revelation: A Radical Synthesis of Science and Spirituality*, Select Books, New York, 2018, p. 31.
3. Rohr, Richard, *The Wisdom Pattern: Order, Chaos, Reorder* (p. 72). Franciscan Media. Kindle Edition.
4. Paul Levy, *The Quantum Revelation*, p. 29.
5. *Ibid.*, p. 29.
6. Lothar Schafer, *Infinite Potential: What Quantum Physics Reveals about How We Should Live*, Deepak Chopra Publisher, 2013, p. 302.
7. *Ibid.*, p. 268.
8. *Ibid.*, p. 282.
9. Cynthia Bourgeault, *The Wisdom Way of Knowing: Reclaiming an Ancient Tradition to Awaken the Heart*, Jossey-Bass Publishing, 2003, p. 27.
10. *Ibid.*, pp., 31-32.
11. "Awe and Wonder in Scientific Practice: Implications for the Relationship Between Science and Religion," Helen De Cruz, www.helendecruz.net, 202=15.
12. Carson, R. "Help Your Child to Wonder," *Woman's Home Companion*, July, 1956: 24–48.
13. Chris Hedges, *The World as It Is: Dispatches on the Myth of Human Progress*, Bold Type Books, 2011, p. 100
14. Zachary Stein, *Covid 19: A War Broke Out in Heaven.*

16. EVOLVE AND DIE: BECOMING A STUDENT OF ENDINGS

1. Stephen Jenkinson, *Die Wise: A Manifesto for Sanity and Soul*, North Atlantic, 2015, p. 13.
2. Cynthia Bourgeault, *The Wisdom Way of Knowing: Reclaiming an Ancient Tradition to Awaken the Heart*, p. 56.
3. Kathleen Dowling Singh, *The Grace in Dying*, Harper One, 2000, p. 124.
4. *The End of Suburbia*, 2004, YouTube, https://www.youtube.com/watch?v=Q3uvzcY2Xug
5. "Deep Adaptation: A Map for Navigating Climate Tragedy," Jem Bendell, https://www.lifeworth.com/deepadaptation.pdf
6. *To You: Zen Sayings of Kodo Sawaki*, Hohm Press, 2021, p. 23.
7. "What a Good Death Is Not," Reena Lazar, https://willoweol.com/what-a-good-death-is-not/
8. Stephen Jenkinson, *Die Wise*, p. 221.

9. Cynthia Bourgeault, *The Wisdom Way of Knowing: Reclaiming an Ancient Tradition to Awaken the Heart*, p. 72.

17. THE AUDACITY OF JOY

1. Rainer Maria Rilke, *Letters on Life*, edited and translated by Ulrich Baer, Modern Library, 2006, p. 175.
2. "We Were Made For These Times," Clarissa Pinkola Estes, https://www.awakin.org/v2/read/view.php?tid=2195
3. Barbara Ehrenreich, "Happy Now?" *John Hopkins Magazine*, September 3, 2010, http://archive.magazine.jhu.edu/2010/09/happy-now/
4. Richard Rohr, *Falling Upward: A Spirituality for the Two Halves of Life*, Josey-Bass, 2011, p. 117.
5. Jung, Carl, *Memories, Dreams, and Reflections*, pp. 451–452.

18. AT HOME AS A REFUGEE

1. "Doing Our Inner Work," Unitarian Universalist Association, https://www.uua.org/new-england/spiritual-leadership/inner-work
2. Jung, Carl, *Collected Works*, Vol. 12, par. 126 (p. 99) Psychology and Alchemy (1952)
3. Zachary Stein, *Covid 19: A War Broke Out in Heaven*.
4. "Climate crisis could displace 1.2bn people by 2050, report warns," Jon Henley, September 9, 2020, https://www.theguardian.com/environment/2020/sep/09/climate-crisis-could-displace-12bn-people-by-2050-report-warns
5. "Liminal Space," Richard Rohr, July 7, 2016, CAC Daily Meditations, https://cac.org/liminal-space-2016-07-07/
6. Zachary Stein, *Covid 19, A War Broke Out In Heaven*.
7. "The Origins of Baptism," *Living Myth Podcast*, Michael Meade, https://www.mosaicvoices.org/episode-268-the-origins-of-baptism
8. Mark Nepo, *Things That Join the Sea and the Sky: Field Notes on Living:* Sounds True, 2017, p. 111.

19. A CULTURE DECOMPENSATING INTO PSYCHOSIS

1. "Jung On Delusions," *Jungian Center for Spiritual Sciences*, https://jungiancenter.org/jung-on-delusion/#_ftnref60
2. "American Psychosis: Trumpism and the Nightmare of History," W.J.T. Mitchell, *Los Angeles Review of Books*, February 16, 2017, https://

lareviewofbooks.org/article/american-psychosis-trumpism-and-the-nightmare-of-history/

3. "This Is What Civilization Ending Feels Like," Umair Haque, *Medium.Com*, February 2, 2022, https://eand.co/this-is-what-a-civilization-ending-feels-like-a7be28d47f86

4. "The War on History Is a War on Democracy," Timothy Snyder, *New York Times*, June 29, 2021, https://www.nytimes.com/2021/06/29/magazine/memory-laws.html

5. "What Can We Learn from the Germans about Confronting Our History?" Lizzie Widdicombe, *New Yorker*, October 21, 2019, https://www.newyorker.com/culture/cultural-comment/what-can-we-learn-from-the-germans-about-confronting-our-history

6. "COVID-19 and PTSD: Assessing the Pandemic's Toll on Mental Health," *Yale School of Medicine*, January, 2022, https://medicine.yale.edu/news-article/covid-19-and-ptsd-assessing-the-pandemics-toll-on-mental-health/

7. "The gun numbers: just 3% of American adults own a collective 133m firearms," *Guardian*, November 15, 2017, https://www.theguardian.com/us-news/2017/nov/15/the-gun-numbers-just-3-of-american-adults-own-a-collective-133m-firearms

8. "Poll: 60 percent of Americans own guns for 'personal safety,'" November 13, 2020, https://www.kwtx.com/2020/11/13/poll-60-percent-of-americans-own-guns-for-personal-safety/

9. "How Will America Finish Collapsing?" Umair Haque, *Medium.Com*, January 24, 2022, https://eand.co/how-will-america-finish-collapsing-ed970339d184

10. "Jung on Delusions," op. cit.

11. "Is America experiencing mass psychosis?" Nicole Karlis, *Salon Magazine*, December 14, 2021, https://www.salon.com/2021/12/14/is-america-experiencing-mass-psychosis/

12. Ibid.

13. *Ibid.*

14. "Finding Our Way by Falling," Michael Meade, *Living Myth Podcast*, Mosaic Voices, https://www.mosaicvoices.org/episode-264-finding-our-way-by-falling

PART II

1. George Orwell, *1984*. Part 2, Chapter 2. Winston explains to Julia how he is able to persevere and stand above the influence of the Party's power.

2. Ann Belford Ulanov, *The Unshuttered Heart: Opening to Aliveness/Deadness in the Self* (Abingdon Press: 2007), 15–16, 17.

20. THE BAD GUYS ARE WINNING

1. "The Bad Guys Are Winning," Anne Applebaum, *The Atlantic*, November 15, 2021, https://www.theatlantic.com/magazine/archive/2021/12/the-autocrats-are-winning/620526/
2. "At This Point, If You're Not Antifa, You're Fa," Tim Wise, *Medium.com*, December 17, 2021, https://timjwise.medium.com/at-this-point-if-youre-not-antifa-you-re-fa-a5973af8ce4c
3. Neil de Grasse Tyson, Twitter, July 18, 2014, https://twitter.com/neiltyson/status/490155821150375937
4. "Climate Change Means Profits for Some, Meaningful Action for Few," NYC Studios, April 1, 2014, https://www.wnycstudios.org/podcasts/takeaway/segments/climate-change-means-profits-some-action-few
5. *Ibid.*
6. "Climate denial is waning on the right. What's replacing it might be just as scary," Oliver Milman, *Guardian*, November 21, 2021, https://www.theguardian.com/environment/2021/nov/21/climate-denial-far-right-immigration
7. *Ibid.*
8. "How authoritarians, despots and 'autocrats' are prevailing all over the world," Alex Henderson, Alternet, November 15, 2021, https://www.alternet.org/2021/11/how-authoritarians-despots-and-autocrats-are-prevailing-all-over-the-world-journalist/
9. "The Trump Coup: Maybe We Can't Handle the Truth," David Corn, *Mother Jones*, February 10, 2022, https://www.motherjones.com/politics/2022/02/the-trump-coup-maybe-we-cant-handle-the-truth/
10. *Ibid.*

21. ROLE MODELS OF JUSTICE AND COURAGE

1. Rachel Carson, *Silent Spring*, Houghton-Mifflin, 1962, p. 44.
2. "Address by Nelson Mandela, Deputy President of the African National Congress (ANC), at the religious service at the Cathedral of Uppsala, Uppsala – Sweden," March 13, 1990, http://www.mandela.gov.za/mandela_speeches/1990/900313_uppsala.htm
3. Aleksandr Solzhenitsyn, *The Gulag Archipelago: 1918-1956, Volume 2*, pp. 615-617.
4. "Themis, The Goddess of Justice," *ThoughtCo*, https://www.thoughtco.com/about-us-4779650
5. "Pursuit of Happiness," Viktor Frankl, https://www.pursuit-of-happiness.org/history-of-happiness/viktor-frankl/
6. Viktor Frankl, *Man's Search for Meaning*, p. 91.
7. Arendt, Hannah. *The Origins of Totalitarianism* (Harvest Book Book 244). HMH Books, preface.

NOTES

8. "All That Is Given: Hanna Arendt on Being Jewish," *Boston Review*, June, 2012, https://bostonreview.net/articles/vivian-gornick-hannah-arendt-on-being-jewish/

9. "Bonhoeffer, Pacifism and Assassination," Mitchell Lewis, 2007, https://milewis.wordpress.com/2007/10/29/bonhoeffer-pacifism-and-assassination/

10. "A Nazi Era Dissident's Reflections on Stupidity Hold Lessons for BJP Supporters," Rohit Kumar, *The Wire*, November 12, 2021, https://thewire.in/society/dietrich-bonhoeffer-nazi-bjp-india-propaganda

11. Dietrich Bonhoeffer, "On Stupidity," *Letters and Papers from Prison* (Dietrich Bonhoeffer Works) Paperback – November 1, 2015, p 103.

12. Dietrich Bonhoeffer, *The Cost of Discipleship*, Touchstone, August, 2021, p. 182.

13. "Sophie Scholl: Student who resisted Hitler and inspires Germany," *BBC*, May 9, 2021, https://www.bbc.com/news/world-europe-57008360

14. "Why did Nelson Mandela go to prison, how long did he spend on Robben Island and Pollsmoor and when was he released?" *UK Sun*, July 18, 2019, https://www.thesun.co.uk/news/6575640/nelson-mandela-prison-how-long-robben-island-pollsmoor-when-released/

15. "Nelson Mandela dies aged 95 – 5 December 2013," *Guardian*, December 6, 2013, https://www.theguardian.com/world/2013/dec/05/nelson-mandela-dies-aged-95-live-updates

16. "A Selection of Quotes from the Late Nelson Mandela," https://www.nelsonmandela.org/content/page/a-selection-of-nelson-mandela-quotes

17. *An Interrupted Life: The Diaries of Etty Hillesum 1941-43*, translated from the Dutch by Arnold J. Pomerans

18. Etty Hillesum, *Letters From Westerbork*, Pantheon Books; 1st edition (November 12, 1986), p. 84.

19. Etty Hillesum, *An Interrupted Life: The Diaries, 1941–1943 and Letters from Westerbork* (New York: Holt, 1996), 3.

20. "Etty Hillesum: *God, Sex, and Defiance in a Time of War,*" Fiona Alison Duncan, *Literary Hub*, September 27, 2017.

21. Etty Hillesum, *An Interrupted Life: The Diaries, 1941-1943; and Letters from Westerbork*, p.83.

22. "Industrial and Agricultural Interests Fight Back," *Environment and Society*, https://www.environmentandsociety.org/exhibitions/rachel-carsons-silent-spring/industrial-and-agricultural-interests-fight-back

23. Lear, Linda (1997). *Rachel Carson: Witness for Nature*. New York: Henry Holt and Company, p. 429.

24. Smith, Michael (Autumn 2011). "'Silence, Miss Carson!' Science, Gender, and the Reception of 'Silent Spring,'" *Feminist Studies*. 27 (3): 733–752.
   "Industrial and Agricultural Interests Fight Back," *Environment and Society*, https://www.environmentandsociety.org/exhibitions/rachel-carsons-silent-spring/industrial-and-agricultural-interests-fight-back

25. "The Writing of "Silent Spring": Rachel Carson and the Culture-Shifting Courage to Speak Inconvenient Truth to Power," *The Marginalian*, https://

www.themarginalian.org/2017/01/27/rachel-carson-silent-spring-dorothy-freeman/

26. Ibid.
27. "Harvesting the Gifts of the Ancestors," Joanna Macy, Molly Young Brown, http://sage-ing.org/wp-content/uploads/ConcertHarvestingtheGiftsoftheAncestorsRevised.pdf

22. ARTIFICIAL INTELLIGENCE: IT'S PERSONAL

1. Shoshana Zuboff, *The Age of Surveillance Capitalism: The Fight for a Human Future at the New Frontier of Power*, Public Affairs, 2019, p.224.
2. "It's not that we've failed to rein in Facebook and Google. We've not even tried," Shoshana Zuboff, *Guardian*, July 2, 2019, https://www.theguardian.com/commentisfree/2019/jul/02/facebook-google-data-change-our-behaviour-democracy
3. "You Are Now Remotely Controlled," Shoshana Zuboff, *New York Times*, January 24, 2020, https://www.nytimes.com/2020/01/24/opinion/sunday/surveillance-capitalism.html
4. "Our attention spans are suffering. Maybe there's a way to get them back," Angela Haupt, *Washington Post*, January 22, 2022, https://www.washingtonpost.com/books/2022/01/22/stolen-focus-johann-hari-book/
5. *Ibid.*
6. "Review of Shoshana Zuboff's *The Age of Surveillance Capitalism*," Erik Larson, *Expensivity*, May 31, 2021, https://www.expensivity.com/erik-j-larson-reviews-surveillance-capitalism/
7. "Shoshana Zuboff: 'Surveillance capitalism is an assault on human autonomy,'" Joanna Kavenna, *Guardian*, October 4, 2019, https://www.theguardian.com/books/2019/oct/04/shoshana-zuboff-surveillance-capitalism-assault-human-automomy-digital-privacy
8. "Mind Reading and Mind Control Technologies Are Coming," *Scientific American*, March 10, 2020, https://blogs.scientificamerican.com/observations/mind-reading-and-mind-control-technologies-are-coming/
9. "Shoshana Zuboff on Surveillance Capitalism's Threat to Democracy," Noah Kulwin, *New York Magazine*, February 24, 2019, https://nymag.com/intelligencer/2019/02/shoshana-zuboff-q-and-a-the-age-of-surveillance-capital.html

23. RESISTING TYRANNY

1. "Not Retreat But Resistance and Resilience: When Faced With Doomsday, Look to Community," Frida Berrigan, *Common Dreams*, February 6, 2022,

https://www.commondreams.org/views/2022/02/06/not-retreat-resistance-and-resilience-when-faced-doomsday-look-community

2. "Donald Trump's ex-wife once said Trump kept a book of Hitler's speeches by his bed," *Business Insider*, September 1, 2015, https://www.businessinsider.com/donald-trumps-ex-wife-once-said-he-kept-a-book-of-hitlers-speeches-by-his-bed-2015-8

3. "Trump praised Hitler to chief of staff John Kelly during Europe trip, new book claims," Dan Mangan, CNBC, July 7, 2021, https://www.cnbc.com/2021/07/07/trump-praised-hitler-to-john-kelly-new-book-claims.html

4. "Twenty Lessons on Fighting Tyranny from the Twentieth Century," *Scholars Strategy Network*, https://scholars.org/contribution/twenty-lessons-fighting-tyranny-twentieth-century

5. "Autocracy: Rules For Survival," Masha Gessen, *New York Review of Books*, November 10, 2016, https://www.nybooks.com/daily/2016/11/10/trump-election-autocracy-rules-for-survival/?lp_txn_id=1325428

6. "Ruth Ben-Ghiat on Coronavirus and the Rise of Autocracy," *Institute for Advanced Study*, 2020, https://www.ias.edu/ideas/ben-ghiat-coronavirus-autocracy

24. HUMANITY'S RITE OF PASSAGE

1. "Between Two Worlds," Malidoma Somé, *Natural Learning*, July, 2010, https://ifnaturallearning.com/resources/540-2/

2. "Is the Modern Psyche Undergoing a Rite of Passage?" Richard Tarnas, https://www.researchgate.net/publication/237378499_Is_the_Modern_Psyche_Undergoing_a_Rite_of_Passage, p. 23

25. GRACE: A BRIEF COMMUNION WITH THE FRAGILITY OF LIFE

1. "Suffering as Grace: An Interview with Ram Dass," Cat Saunders, *Sun Magazine*, December 1990, https://www.thesunmagazine.org/issues/181/suffering-as-grace

2. Richard Rohr, *Everything Belongs*, Crossroad Publishing, 2015, p. 18.

3. "'Grace Without God' explores life in America without religion," Heidi Stevens, *Chicago Tribune*, June 27, 2016, https://www.chicagotribune.com/columns/heidi-stevens/ct-grace-without-god-book-balancing-0627-20160627-column.html

4. Mark Nepo, *The Book of Awakening: Having the Life You Want by Being Present to the Life You Have*, Conari Press, 2011, pp. 246-47.

5. "The Fourfold Grace of Won Buddhism," Doyeon Park, *Lion's Roar*, March 4, 2020, https://www.lionsroar.com/fourfold-grace-won-buddhism/

NOTES

6. The Center for Courage and Renewal, "The Meanings of Grace," Pema Chodron, http://www.couragerenewal.org/PDFs/CourageRenewal-Meanings-of-Grace.pdf

7. "The Bones of Grace," Mark Nepo, *Patheos*, August 7, 2017, https://www.patheos.com/blogs/fieldnotesonliving/2017/08/07/the-bones-of-grace/

8. Machado de Oliveira, Vanessa. *Hospicing Modernity*, North Atlantic Books, p. 235.

9. *Ibid.*, p. 238.

10. Zach Stein, Covid 19: A War Broke Out In Heaven.

AFTERWORD

1. Carl Jung, *Collected Works*, Vol. 5, Paragraph 553.

ABOUT THE AUTHOR

Carolyn Baker, Ph.D., was a psychotherapist in private practice for seventeen years and a professor of psychology and history for ten. She is the author of fifteen books, including *Navigating the Coming Chaos: A Handbook for Inner Transition; Sacred Demise: Walking the Spiritual Path of Industrial Civilization's Collapse*; and *Love in the Age of Ecological Apocalypse*. She has also co-authored four books with Andrew Harvey. She manages her website at www.carolynbaker.net and publishes a subscription-based *Daily News Digest* which is a collection of news stories and inspiration focusing on the global crisis and options for navigating disruptive times.

Carolyn offers life coaching and spiritual counseling for people who want help with navigating the unprecedented challenges of our time.

Carolyn may be contacted at Carolyn@carolynbaker.net.

Made in the USA
Las Vegas, NV
09 September 2022

54976335R00132